Penguin

Why the one you fancy never fancies *you*

Richard Robinson is the author of seven books on popular science, including *Why the Toast Always Lands Butter Side Down* and the Science Magic series (Oxford University Press), which was shortlisted for the Aventis Prize. He works full-time as a science presenter, and regularly performs demonstrations around the world from Boston to Beijing. He was also a founder member of the satirical ITV series *Spitting Image*.

Also by Richard Robinson

Why the Toast Always Lands Butter Side Down

Why the one you fancy never fancies *you*

Richard Robinson

PENGUIN BOOKS

PENGUIN BOOKS

Published by the Penguin Group
Penguin Group (Australia)
250 Camberwell Road, Camberwell, Victoria 3124, Australia
(a division of Pearson Australia Group Pty Ltd)
Penguin Group (USA) Inc.
375 Hudson Street, New York, New York 10014, USA
Penguin Group (Canada)
90 Eglinton Avenue East, Suite 700, Toronto ON M4P 2Y3, Canada
(a division of Pearson Penguin Canada Inc.)
Penguin Books Ltd
80 Strand, London WC2R 0RL England
Penguin Ireland
25 St Stephen's Green, Dublin 2, Ireland
(a division of Penguin Books Ltd)
Penguin Books India Pvt Ltd
11 Community Centre, Panchsheel Park, New Delhi – 110 017, India
Penguin Group (NZ)
67 Apollo Drive, Rosedale, North Shore 0632 New Zealand
(a division of Pearson New Zealand Ltd)
Penguin Books (South Africa) (Pty) Ltd
24 Sturdee Avenue, Rosebank, Johannesburg 2196, South Africa

Penguin Books Ltd, Registered Offices: 80 Strand, London, WC2R 0RL, England

First published by Constable & Robinson Ltd, 2006
This edition published by Penguin Group (Australia), 2007

1 3 5 7 9 10 8 6 4 2

Text copyright © Richard Robinson 2006

The moral right of the author has been asserted

Cover design by Nikki Townsend © Penguin Group (Australia)
Illustrations by Kate Charlesworth
Page 53 Wodaabe males at the annual Geerewol festival © Carol Beckwith/Angela Fisher/photokunst;
Page 55 *The Judgement of Paris*, by Peter Paul Rubens, National Gallery, London/The Bridgeman Art Gallery.

Printed and bound in Australia by McPherson's Printing Group, Maryborough, Victoria

National Library of Australia
Cataloguing-in-Publication data:

Robinson, Richard, 1950– .
Why the one you fancy never fancies you : Murphy's laws of love.
Bibliography.
ISBN 978 0 14 300692 3.
1. Love. 2. Interpersonal relations. 3. Murphy's law. I. Title.

158.2

penguin.com.au

To the Bennett-Houlton household,
Leonie, Simon and Miriam

CONTENTS

INTRODUCTION

Murphy's Laws work for most things. They work double-plus for personal relationships because the driving force behind the laws is passion, same as the driving force behind love. All the laws here are best read with a heavy sigh of exasperation.

WHATEVER CAN GO WRONG WILL GO WRONG.

Murphy's Laws of love are all pessimistic, of course. Everything goes wrong, nothing ever goes right. No happy ending. The one you fancy continuously refuses to fancy you whatever charms, potions or spells you employ. Meanwhile, you are being stalked all day by someone who will *not* stop pestering you. The logo for the book should be an eternal triangle, in which everyone fancies someone who fancies someone else, who fancies . . .

But away with gloom. There is a winsome, war-weary chirpy kind of bonhomie throughout these Murphy's Laws. The spirit of the bomb shelter is here. The darling of the forces is singing:

We'll meet again, don't know where, don't know when,
But I know we'll meet again, some sunny day.
I'll text you next week sometime, maybe.

We know we're all doomed, but for some reason we are compelled to throw ourselves at the enemy again and again and again.

Chapter 1, Roll, Pitch and Yaw, looks at *you*, because if we're going to look at 'you and them', we ought to pop a glance at *you* before getting to grips with *them* – and *you* are not that easy to see. In fact, let's face it, we're all a little fuzzy at the edges. We're not entirely certain about our identity. One reason for that is outlined in Chapter 1, and is central to the book – we use 'mirror neurons' in our brains to reflect the outside world. Our internal self-image is created from these reflections. Some of those reflections are the opinions of others, which we reflect back to them, and they back to us, and back and forth, and back and forth, which accounts for the fuzziness. Your three main influences, or mirrors, are your family, your friends and your genes. We see how they mix to make you *you*.

Chapter 2, Men and Women: Gulf Wars, looks at 'them'; what makes the opposite sex tick. We imagine there is a gigantic difference between men and women, and all Murphy's Laws are based on this brutishly simplistic Punch and Judy show. The laws selected here are among the most tame, though you wouldn't know by looking. They do, however, reveal something interesting about the way we assess the world. We are all 'difference engines', almost incapable of accurate measurement but happy to compare one thing with another. To make the comparison easier we enhance the differences. Whether we are distinguishing between colours, races or sexes, the smallest difference is magnified in our minds to make it more manageable. It isn't anything political or pathological, just practical. Our difference engine has evolved to make life simpler. The more important a thing is to us, the more differences we notice. For instance, the Eskimos famously have thirty-two words for what the rest of us call 'snow'. We have 32,000 words for the opposite sex, not all of them printable.

Chapter 3, Courting Disaster, sends you out in pursuit of love. Here we look at the exhausting amount of acting that has to go on in courtship. All the kit and caboodle, the fluff and kerfuffle. Our guide through this section is the greatest thespian in the animal world, the bower bird. He shows us how to copy fashion and steal ideas from others to make the very best impression on prospective partners. We also pause to scratch our heads at the peacock, a bird so well dressed it cripples him. Are we any better than these two?

Chapter 4, Nice Assessment, is for people who are still in pursuit of the perfect partner. What judgements do we use to assess possible partners? Not very clever ones, it seems. Here we find that the visual similarity of the brain to a pile of sausages is more than just superficial. We habitually think with sausage-logic. Most women, it is said, select their husband in lighting they would not choose a car by. Stephen Leacock said 'many a man in love with a dimple makes the mistake of marrying the whole girl'. We are all guilty of bad calls occasionally.

We do occasionally apply sensible rules in choosing mates. Quite pragmatic and sane they are, although so easily overtaken by chance and whim. For instance, research has shown that the second most important thing girls look for in a man is a steady income, because that will be useful for any child they may have. That is good sense, isn't it? So if that is the second thing they look for, what is the first? Sexiness! That, as the next section shows, sinks good sense beneath the waves.

Chapter 5, Slithery Slopes, deals with hormones, the real boss of the organization. We have kept away from hormones until now, because once they come into the picture, everything else fades in significance to nothing. The section on the evolution of emotions, on pp. 173–7, gives some of the reasons why hormones rule and ruled for 3.5 billion years before we appeared on the planet. In spite of this, not a lot is known about how they work. They are complicated molecules, which doesn't help our under-standing, but the main reason we know so little is rather more mundane: most science research is driven by industry, which isn't very interested in funding experiments into the meaning of love, so probing our emotions is done between more lucrative jobs. This is neat: investigations into recre-ational activities carried out during recreation time.

Chapter 6, The Nitty Gritty, finds you in bed with your loved one at last. Now, this is not a sex manual. No interest-ing new positions or craftily engineered gadgets to be found here. This is soft science, so we will be looking at the biology, the psychology and the anthropology of it all. Still, I bring interesting tales of the strange discoveries of science, from the 1,000 kg (2,205 lb) testicles to the crea-ture with 11,000 penises.

Chapter 7, Wedding Prescience, catapults you out of bed, towards the altar and into marriage. The custom of marriage, with all its rituals, social networks and legal obligations, is uniquely human. The only time that animals have formal marriages is when they wed humans, which is reassuringly rare. The Roman Emperor Caligula is often said to have both married his horse Incitatus and in a fit of nepotism appointed it to the Senate. In 2005 Sharon Tendle married a dolphin, Cindy, and in 2006 a Sudanese man was ordered by the courts to marry a goat following sexual activity with it. In this section we will focus on humans, who can nonetheless behave like animals on occasions.

Chapter 8, Playing Away, pops you out the other end of marriage, via rumour and scandal, disgrace, misery and remorse – the usual thing. Just as a scientific book should do, we study infidelity with statistical rigour and find that it happens; something which nevertheless always surprises and shocks us. Marriages are always entered into with the full armada of hopes and best wishes from everyone, but if we looked harder at the statistics maybe we would all have prenups as well as good wishes. Prenuptial agreements provide for the division of property in the event of separation. Considering that separation is the conclusion of a third of marriages in the West, should prenups be compulsory? That is out of the question, of course! That would take all the thrill out of marriage, like trying to ride the roller-coaster with the brakes firmly on.

Chapter 9, The Wheel Turns Full Circle, sees you do it all over again. Straight after one crashed relationship, you can't wait to have another go on the roller-coaster of love. Murphy's Laws are fully in support of the second marriage. Whatever can go wrong will go wrong, and will do so repeatedly if given the chance.

ROLL, PITCH AND YAW

So here you are, just about to sweep out of the house, slamming the door behind you (again). What brought you to this point? Whose fault is it your life is in ruins (again)? It's the parents, isn't it? They are so fussy, so bad-tempered all the time. Nag, nag, nag. Can't they see you are old enough to look after yourself now? You're FIFTEEN, FOR CHRISSAKES!

But still they keep buzzing around. 'Did you count the tent-pegs, because you don't want to be caught in a storm with a tent that blows away and why did you leave it until the last minute to renew your passport you'll be too late one day and then you'll be sorry you must remember to keep *all* receipts and you know the one time you don't wear a cycle helmet is the one time you'll fall off and please don't stay out so late again and please phone and it's lunchtime shouldn't you be out of bed and surely you're not going out in THAT you'll catch your death . . .'

OK. That's IT. When you were young they could have their way with you. From now on things are going to be different.

'I'm outa here.'

'You are so ungrateful,' they say. 'After all we've done for you.'

'You treat me like a child all the time. Why can't you treat me like a grown-up?'

'When you start behaving like a grown-up we'll start treating you like a grown-up!'

SLAM!!! So satisfying, that sound. But where are you going next? Come to that, who are you?

The real you

This section is about finding out who the 'real you' is. As you can see by the fact that this chapter isn't five volumes long, we aren't going to get anywhere near you really, but we can look at your three important components.

When you look in the mirror every morning, who do you see? Pretty one day, ugly the next; fit yesterday, fat today. What you are looking at is more than a simple reflection, it's a composite drawn from three sources: you, your family and your circle of friends.

As an analogy, it's rather like flying a plane, with three forces to worry about: **roll** (tilting left or right), **pitch** (tipping upwards or downwards) and **yaw** (heading left or right). Your friends decide your roll, your family control your pitch, and your YOU is fighting to steady the yaw. If your mum says you're clever, that adjusts your pitch. If your best friend decides to tell you how selfish you are, that alters your roll. If you write a really hot song, your yaw changes. Aeronautics experts call the combination of these three 'attitude', so the analogy is a good one. When the

happy day comes that you finally have the right attitude, in harmony with your co-pilots, you will probably find you are twenty-five years old. Until then you are mostly in tail-spin. And when you look in the mirror every morning you find there's a different pilot.

CALL IT A CLAN, CALL IT A NETWORK, CALL IT A TRIBE, CALL IT A FAMILY. WHATEVER YOU CALL IT, WHOEVER YOU ARE, YOU NEED ONE.

(Jane Howard)

Your family – PITCH

How much of 'you' is your distinctive, original self that you were born with, your essence, spirit or soul? How much is the result of your parents fiddling about with you for the past fifteen years? The essential you – the genetic you – is very evident from the moment you enter the world, as anyone who is present at the birth will testify, because all babies are different. We also know more than ever before that the nurturing environment of your family is a very strong influence. You have been bonded to your parents to an incredible degree since you were born. Proof of this came in 1995 with the discovery of mirror neurons.

Mirror neurons

Neuroscientist Giacomo Rizzolatti, working with fMRI scanners, discovered that the brain of one person mirrors the brain of another. When A watches B doing something,

A's brain fires in exactly the same way as B's. The immediate effect of this is that A is automatically thinking the same thoughts as B. You could call it 'empathy', the ability to feel another's pain or share their joy. But the problem with that word is that it implies you could control it; you could *choose* to empathize or not. In fact you can't control mirror neurons: the learning process is almost automatic. You pick up the aura, the style, the flavour of your family and incorporate it, without giving it a serious thought. The question of whether you 'love' Mum and Dad hardly comes into it – you are part of them, as they are part of you: you are psychically inseparable.

I DON'T HAVE TO LOOK UP MY FAMILY TREE, BECAUSE I KNOW THAT I'M THE SAP.

(Fred Allen)

Can you manage without a family?

The family environment is the first thing to be absorbed by the infant, via mirror neurons. The rituals and routines are so much a part of daily life that it can come as a complete surprise later to find that other families are different. If you are used to saying prayers at the start of meals you can't imagine a home where they don't. It is strangely worrying to visit a household that just gets down to eating at meal-times; there's something missing somehow, and you may find yourself whispering grace privately to yourself at the start of tea.

On the other hand, if your parents are on the Social Services danger list – always screaming at each other and at you – how strangely quiet is the family that doesn't scream. It isn't necessarily comforting for a young child to find herself in a quiet home. She has incorporated her own special family style at a deep level, and can be unnerved by strange new ways. Social Services are very chary about removing children from their home environment, even where families seem so dysfunctional that the child could be in danger. You might take them away and give them peace, attention and mountains of material improvements, yet they will still remain in mourning for a long time. The family bond is deep and strong.

WE ARE FACED WITH INSURMOUNTABLE OPPORTUNITIES!

(Charlie Brown)

Your friends – ROLL

You have slammed the door on your family. You have shaken off the petty rules and restrictions of home. You are free at last!

Well, not actually. Truth be told, you are diving into a new kind of bondage – new rules, restrictions, customs, traditions and orthodoxies – this time created by your friends. Adolescents are the most conventional, rule-bound people of all. They may be busy rebelling at home, but there's no rebellion out in town. Strict dress code is enforced, whether in your own group or to impress the opposite sex. All girls must wear the thinnest things on the coldest evenings. They have to. Their midriffs must be bare, no question. Boys must never ever be seen wearing a tie. Footwear is vetted. Derisive sneers if you wear the wrong sunglasses. Phone fashions are discussed endlessly, until everyone knows the ranking, from phat to skanky.

Without your parents' guiding hand your friends provide their own guiding iron fist, which keeps all members penned into the group. Each group member reflects the others through their mirror neurons, reinforcing conformity with private signals, handshakes and a language all of their own.

Rap lyrics are an example of extreme language, on the cusp of breaking free entirely from the grandmother tongue. We are grateful to an Oakland High School student for this translation of a rap by Notorious B.I.G.

Don't see my ones, don't see my guns – get it
    Now tell ya friends Poppa hit it then split it
In two as I flow with the Junior Mafia
    I don't know what the hell's stoppin' ya
I'm clockin' ya –Versace shades watchin' ya
    Once ya grin, I'm in game, begin

Translation: Understand this fact: you can have neither my money, nor my weapons. I suggest that you inform your peers that we engaged in violent sexual acts. Currently, I am rapping with my associates, the Junior Mafia. I'm having some difficulty understanding why you refuse to approach me. I am attempting to make eye contact with you through my expensive glasses, and as soon as you respond with a smile, I will approach you.

CUSTOM MEETS US AT THE CRADLE AND LEAVES US ONLY AT THE TOMB.

(Robert Ingersoll)

Customs and rituals

The customs and rituals of your mates help bond the group together. Group bonding is a central feature of humanity, as it is for our cousins the chimpanzees (and for our great great, great . . . great grandparents, the amoebas; see p. 174). Chimps stick together for safety and work together to raise the young, forage and hunt. The group is ten times more effective than any individual could be. The tribe is structured: usually one principal male with subordinates ranked below him. The females play their part in controlling the males, as well as rearing and disciplining the juniors. The bonding is reinforced by mutual grooming. The rituals that chimps use could be called their 'customs', although they are less complex than ours. Nevertheless, if an ape breaks with the customs – behaves badly in the opinion of the tribe – he is ostracized.

For an ape to be cast out from the tribe is a sentence of death. The jungle is not a forgiving place. If the outcast is not regularly groomed parasites sap his energy and invite diseases. Other ape tribes will attack him. Predators will gather around the ailing ape and there will be no lookouts or help that can save him.

Around the streets of your neighbourhood a genteel version of the same thing is played out. The group is bonded by customs of language, dress and behaviour. Anyone who breaks badly with the others is ostracized. Dating the wrong girl, being seen with someone else's man, all offenders are punished by being shunned. Being an outcast in the city is not usually as dire as in the jungle; it isn't a death sentence. But if you live in Brixton, Sao Paulo or Harlem you won't want to be out on your own at night. We all need friends.

A BOY BECOMES AN ADULT THREE YEARS BEFORE HIS PARENTS THINK HE DOES, AND ABOUT TWO YEARS AFTER HE THINKS HE DOES.

(Lewis B. Hershey)

Yourself – YAW

What about your YOU? The third component of your 'attitude' is the most puzzling. Modern brain-scanning technology allows us to see what is happening inside your head during adolescence. These changes are invisible, unlike the ones we usually associate with puberty – breasts, hair, height, muscles, etc. – but they are every bit as significant. What we find is a seething mass of growth and change.

While you were busy being a child your brain was growing neurons in profusion to deal with the mass of new experiences while you experimented with the world. From the onset of puberty, however, and for the next decade or so, brain scans show that the neurons begin to decrease in number. At the same time the insulation around them increases. (The insulation comes from fatty myelin cells, which envelop the nerves and make nerve transmission more efficient.) This suggests that the neurons, having experimented with trillions of connections, have selected a few billion which they are now fixing in place with the insulation. The final, glorious you, the perfect you, will emerge when all that work has been done inside your brain.

GROWING PAINS IN OTHER PLACES

The European path through puberty makes you cry a lot less than some. Many cultures around the world mark the onset of puberty by inflicting serious pain in the form of circumcision, sub-incision (you don't want to know about that), scarring, wild boar-wrestling etc. I bet you're glad to be free of all that.

Well . . . not that glad, evidently, since you have a powerful urge to do equally painful things to yourself – face-furniture, tattoos, midwinter midriff-baring. It seems that the rite of passage will be undergone, whether the grown-ups do it or not.

We also find that in poorer countries adolescence doesn't exist. For girls this is most obvious: the gap between reaching sexual maturity and making babies is as short as the local lads can make it. For boys, once the coming-of-age ritual is over they are given their spanner or spear and told to get on with it. So there is no time for teenage crises. Life is too busy, death is too close.

In the West, though, your childhood is kept tucked in the back pocket wherever you go, to be reached for and cuddled in times of confusion.

MY LIFE HAS A SUPERB CAST, BUT I CAN'T FIGURE OUT THE PLOT.

(Ashleigh Brilliant)

Adolescence

But the insulating process doesn't progress evenly, and this is why adolescents behave like adolescents. The centre of the brain is first to be completed, in your mid-teens. This is the part where your emotions spring from – the limbic system. So that means that your emotions are working with great efficiency, running on all cylinders.

The control of the limbic system ought to come from the frontal lobes, which look after tact, decorum, ethics, long-term planning and general good taste. The hitch is

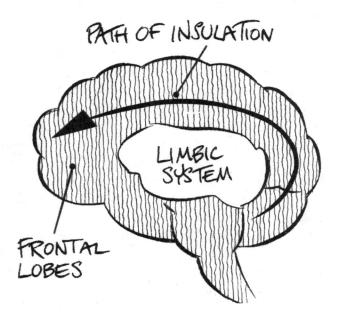

that these lobes are the last to get insulated, since the work progresses from the back of the head towards the front. So for a decade or so your emotions are running away with you, and your controls are incapable of doing anything about it. As the English visionary, William Blake, put it:

The tigers of wrath are stronger than the horses of instruction.

ADOLESCENCE: A STAGE BETWEEN INFANCY AND ADULTERY.

(Ambrose Bierce)

The gap between maturity and parenthood

By the time you reach sixteen you are sexually mature. Maturity varies greatly from person to person, from country to country, with girls generally maturing a couple of years before boys, but that's roughly the mark. Romeo met Juliet when he was sixteen and she fourteen, and Mary probably had Jesus when she was about sixteen, so that was the way the world went until relatively recently.

Nowadays in the West the most popular age for commencing a family is twenty-six. That's an enormous difference. Between sixteen and twenty-six lie ten years which were not at all planned for by evolution. You were designed to make babies as soon as puberty happened. What are you going to do while you're waiting?

Adulthood has been officially deferred because there are some very important jobs to do first. A whole heap of knowledge has to be absorbed so that we can cope with the elaborate world we have created. Ever since the

invention of writing, and then printing, life has been filling up with books, forms, facts and figures, and of course exams, lots of them. Improvements in contraception allow women to choose when to have a child and longer life expectancy means there is less hurry, so they've taken the chance to put off the fateful day.

PUBERTY IN OTHER ANIMALS

In the natural world, generally speaking, the smaller you are, the faster you make babies. Some bacteria can start families on their twentieth birthday – twenty minutes that is. Imagine, if you divide into two every twenty minutes – that is, if the population doubles every twenty minutes – the bacteria can form a lump the size of a sugar cube within a day or so. If allowed to continue at this rate the ball of microbes would be the size of the earth within a week. (Luckily for us the microbial death rate is almost as high as their birth rate.) Larger animals are slower at making babies. The elephant has just one calf every four years.

In most insects the change to maturity happens after a pupa stage, in which the larva seems to go completely quiescent in a thick shell for a few months. Inside, though, they are churning around like a washing machine. Whole organs are disappearing and new ones are formed – their caterpillar eyes dissolve and new compound eyes sprout, along with new legs and wings. The fully grown adult that emerges with a theatrical flourish bears no resemblance to the grub of a few months ago.

Now, if that pupa was compelled to sit at breakfast every morning, as you are, it would feel pretty self-conscious. At the age of fifteen you are like that dissolving grub, with a nose which is expanding so rapidly you can hear it creak, ears that have morphed overnight into satellite dishes, hair creeping out of the strangest places, and the whole lot peppered with ugly pink spots and alien smells. It's hardly surprising you stay holed up in your room for as long as you can. At school you are pupils, at home, pupae.

**A MAN WHO CARRIES A CAT BY THE TAIL
LEARNS SOMETHING HE CAN LEARN IN NO
OTHER WAY.**

(Mark Twain)

The importance of mistakes

In the end the University of Life does practical courses
only. You can only get your 'attitude' right by rolling your

sleeves up, getting stuck in and getting bruised, picking yourself up and starting again. Thomas Edison said he never made mistakes, but he did find 10,000 ways that didn't work. Soichiro Honda, founder of the Honda Motor Corporation, said, 'Success is 99 per cent failure.' In life, as in Honda, you have to try. You just have to. The greatest mistake is to be scared of making a mistake. Evangelist Martyn Lloyd-Jones said, 'To do something and fail is so much better than to do nothing and succeed.' James Joyce, the author, said, 'Mistakes are portals of discovery.'

If you're scared of the stigma of failure, being cool is much safer. Smile, stay back and say nothing. Let others make fools of themselves. Learn nothing, but look good.

EXPERIENCE IS THE NAME EVERYONE GIVES TO HIS MISTAKES.

(Oscar Wilde)

TRY AGAIN. FAIL AGAIN. FAIL BETTER.

(Samuel Beckett)

MEN AND WOMEN: GULF WARS

Before you throw yourself into the battle for sex we should look at the battle of the sexes. Arguments about the differences between men and women are almost as numerous and bitterly fought as those about the differences between humans and apes. It is as if men and women were separate species. As a result, Murphy's Laws are all blatantly sexist. However, they can be used as a starting point for analysing the difference between men and women.

Let's begin by distinguishing between two sorts of sexism: *general* sexism is when a man makes biased remarks about women; *specific* sexism is when a man makes biased remarks about the woman in front of him. You can get away with one, but not with the other. Why? Because there certainly is a difference between men and women on average, but the person opposite is not average, so you shouldn't try it.

The Normal Distribution Curve

To look for possible variations between men and women, scientists have to test hundreds of volunteers, then draw a graph and look for significant differences. The graphs that measure aptitude at things like map-reading, mood-reading, embedded figure tests and so on all have a similar shape. They all end up looking like this:

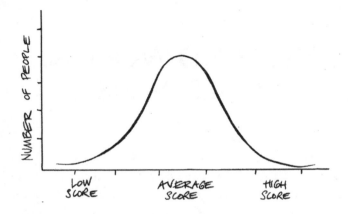

The high point in the middle shows the number of people who are pretty good at it, while the graph tails away to left and right, showing those who are very good or those who are very bad. So we can see that most people are pretty good, while a few are exceptionally good and a few are exceptionally bad. That 'bell curve' or 'normal distribution curve' is indeed normal.

If we plot both men and women on the same graph, measuring, say, map-reading skills, we may get the pair of curves opposite.

This shows that there is a significant difference between men and women, with men, on average, being better at this particular task. However, the graphs overlap so much that we have to conclude that, apart from 15 per cent or so on either side, both sexes perform equally well. So you can talk

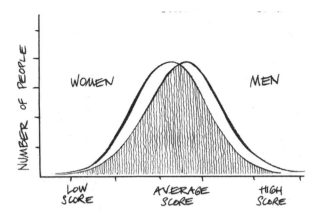

about 'all men do this' and 'all women are like that' only if you understand that an individual man probably doesn't . . . and an individual woman probably isn't . . .

To draw it another way, here's a man and a woman showing the differences (in white); where they overlap (in grey) they are the same.

We don't see it like that, though. We see the differences as total, with a vast gulf separating all women from all men.

Many of the differences in male and female psychology are small and most of them are non-existent, but Murphy's Laws drive a wedge between them.

SPOT THE DIFFERENCE

WOMEN WHO SEEK TO BE EQUAL WITH MEN LACK AMBITION.

(Timothy Leary)

Are there any differences between men and women?

Apart from the very obvious differences between females and males – the differences which started the whole sex thing off in the first place – there are other pretty general qualities, such as height, weight, hairiness and the tendency to fight. Are there any more ways to tell them apart?

Women tend to be vague, naive, pedantic, arrogant, hypercritical, simplistic, childish, petty, argumentative, neurotic, obsessive, clumsy, devious, lazy, untidy and selfish.

Men, on the other hand, are often argumentative, childish, clumsy, obsessive, untidy, selfish, arrogant, pedantic, devious, petty, neurotic, vague, hypercritical, naive, simplistic and lazy.

If you found yourself agreeing with one of those lists and not the other, you are being sexist, since they are both the same list, rearranged.

Meanwhile, we all know people from either side of the gulf who are intelligent, thoughtful, generous, humorous, warm-hearted, caring, enthusiastic, wise and easy-going . . . until they start talking about the opposite sex.

Three factors have made the differences greater than they should be.

1) As they are generally bigger, men are able to impose their will on women. When push comes to shove they can push and shove harder than women. So men have tended to put themselves in positions of power over women.

2) Over the millennia what generally does happen is what we expect to happen. So we legislate on the basis that 'all men do this' and 'all women are like that'.

3) On a daily basis, the differences that do exist between the sexes are exaggerated in our minds. See the next Murphy's Law in particular, and most of the ones that follow.

WOMEN HAVE THEIR FAULTS
MEN HAVE ONLY TWO
EVERYTHING THEY SAY
AND EVERYTHING THEY DO.

The difference engine

This splendid way we divide the world into two helps us to distinguish one thing from another. So it's us and them, yin and yang, Democrats and Republicans, left-wing and right-wing, big-enders and little-enders, heaven and hell, chalk and cheese, with us or agin' us, all or nothing, hero or villain, hard or soft, terrorist or freedom fighter, black or white, winners or losers.

The separation is exaggerated because of a basic part of human psychology: we are difference engines. We don't see things in absolute terms – 'hot', 'dark', 'noisy' – but only by comparing them to the surroundings – 'hotter than...', 'darker than...' The temperature of your local swimming pool is perhaps 28°C (82°F), but it will seem hot or cold, depending on whether you've sneaked a paddle in the hot pool a minute ago, or have just crawled naked through a snowdrift to get to it. A room you walk into may seem gloomy or bright, depending on the one you've just left. Your eye can't automatically calculate the luminance in the way a light meter can.

In the absence of absolute accuracy the brain exaggerates differences to make them seem more extreme. The picture opposite shows two grey squares. You can see one is darker than the other by comparing them where they touch. That border is important. Place your finger along the join and the difference between the squares disappears. Now instead of two grey squares you see one grey oblong. When a difference is perceived it is exaggerated. That's as true for those grey squares as it is for the colourful tapestry of your life.

Another Murphy's Law says it all:

THE WORLD CAN BE DIVIDED INTO TWO SORTS OF PEOPLE: THOSE WHO DIVIDE THE WORLD INTO TWO SORTS OF PEOPLE AND THOSE WHO DON'T.

THREE WISE MEN – ARE YOU SERIOUS?

Should women be put in power?

Politics has been dominated by men for a long time, and for a long time women have said that is a mistake. If men dictate policy, they say, the inevitable result is confrontation, argument and war. Hand the reins of power to women and all will be peace instantly. Men are so pumped up with testosterone, they are bound to fight, while ladies, being so good at empathizing, can chat with other (female) heads of state and sort out the world's problems over a cup of tea.

Setting aside the female world leaders and their attempts to bring global peace (and setting Mrs Thatcher firmly aside), the experience of women managers in business and commerce is that they often show the same qualities of ambitiousness, control, secrecy, evasiveness and envy that men are infamous for. As with men, some women are effective and popular, some are not.

GIVE A WOMAN AN INCH AND SHE THINKS SHE'S A RULER.

Should women be kept away from power?

People – male or female – don't like giving up power. Because of their difference engine they see every tiny concession as a total loss of power. More than that, they see the collapse of civilization looming if they give an inch. The argument for keeping voting rights from women used to be that they would end up voting on petty, domestic issues instead of considering the national interest. (Oh, and they were also genetically inferior, incapable of making up their minds and would vote for anyone with a nice smile.) The world has not collapsed since women got the vote. The difference engines created a gulf between women and men that plainly isn't there.

THE ONLY DIFFERENCE BETWEEN MEN AND BOYS IS THE COST OF THEIR TOYS.

The slight difference

Men have a reputation for being devoted to gadgets, analysing things, sorting things, fiddling with machines, anything that a) gets them playing with objects rather than people and b) turns their back to the rest of the home. The shed was invented for men. There they can sit in silence and wrestle with nice, simple, hard things with hinges, not wobbly, soft things that interrupt, like wives, children, etc.

Psychologists have identified a broad division between men and women. Men are better systematizers, women better empathizers. So men are happier at engineering tasks which need step-by-step logical thinking, while women excel at broader connectivity and human interactions ('web-thinking' against male 'step-thinking', according to anthropologist Helen Fisher).

There might be a common link. Simon Baron-Cohen, in his book *The Essential Difference*, explains how a whole raft of 'typically' male characteristics are linked to one simple thing: a difference in the level of testosterone between males and females. Studying babies' testosterone levels, Baron-Cohen found that baby boys with higher foetal testosterone levels had a smaller vocabulary and made eye contact less often than normal boys when they were a year old. And a study by another group showed that eight-year-old girls who, as foetuses, had high levels of the hormone, performed better than average at tasks such as mentally rotating a two-dimensional figure, normally considered to be a male preserve.

It could be that high foetal testosterone levels push brain development towards an improved ability to see patterns and analyse systems – tasks males tend to be better at. But it also impairs communication and empathy – which are usually more highly developed in females.

IF IT CAN'T BE FIXED BY DUCT TAPE OR WD-40, IT'S A FEMALE PROBLEM.

(Jason Love)

The testosterone link

Testosterone production is what makes the male different from the female in one very important sense: no testes, no testosterone. But why should that same testosterone influence such a range of activities that are nothing to do with maleness as such? There is no particular reason why web-thinking should be the domain of women, or why step-thinking should be a male preserve. It confers no evolutionary advantage. Could it be that this is just an evolutionary accident? A side effect of testosterone? If you have one, you get the other thrown in, whether you want it or not? Love me, love my hobbies?

In other areas there are many examples of one property being linked to another, of one cause having more than one effect. If you want the joy of babies you have to be prepared for the eighteen years that follow. If you want central heating all winter and air conditioning all summer, you're going to have to cope with the global warming which follows. Likewise, it appears that if you want to have males in the house, you are going to have to get used to those toys.

EVERY WOMAN IS WRONG UNTIL SHE CRIES, AND THEN SHE IS RIGHT – INSTANTLY.

(Thomas Chandler Haliburton)

Do men have emotions?

One of the most common generalizations about women is that they are more sensitive and caring than men. Simon Baron-Cohen's evidence would support this – more people skills, more awareness of the feelings of others, is a female attribute.

But only on average. The overlap is so huge, as Baron-Cohen himself stresses, that to legislate on the basis of this difference would be inappropriate. However, in England that is what they have done. Divorced fathers have to battle in the courts to gain access to their children. The legal system's natural default state is that men have no idea which end of a baby is which, can't cook or tidy, and will never be able to bond successfully with the child. This may be true on average, but trying to persuade the magistrate that she is not dealing with an average man is near-impossible at the present time.

It should come as no surprise that when men are given the task of rearing children they do it with exactly the same skill and verve as women, and with the same hardness, softness, pleasure, frustration and devotion. The difference is mythical.

SURE GOD CREATED MAN BEFORE WOMAN. BUT THEN YOU ALWAYS MAKE A ROUGH DRAFT BEFORE THE FINAL MASTERPIECE.

Which came first, men or women?

It would appear that the Bible story had it the wrong way round. The female came first. Early life on earth was a cell which simply split down the middle every now and then. This was asexual reproduction, and asexual reproduction is an all-egg event. No romantic dinners and bedtime frolics here. Some millions of years later an amoeba began to shuffle its DNA before splitting in two. This was sexual reproduction, but not as we know it; there was still no bloke involved. It was all done in-house, as it were. The next stage of sexual evolution was the shuffling of DNA from two packs – creatures were hermaphrodite, possessing both male and female gametes. This was good; it produced

THE SISTERINE CHAPEL

much useful genetic variation, the very stuff of evolution. By the time the first distinctive male happened along evolution on earth was well under way; the first male was probably something like a frog (which puts the old fairy tale about princesses and frog-kissing into perspective; see p. 65). The distinctive Y-chromosome, which is what makes a male a male, was an even later development. So girls came first. Whether that means that Man is therefore the final masterpiece is less certain.

NEVER ARGUE WITH A WOMAN WHEN SHE'S TIRED – OR RESTED.

Why women nag

Is there a gene for nagging? There's probably a bloke somewhere peering down his microscope, searching the X-chromosome for it, on the basis that 'only women do it, so it must be sex-determined'. The reputation women have as

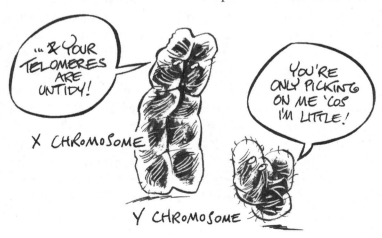

nags goes back to ancient Greek comedies. In medieval Europe the ducking stools were used principally for cooling 'scolds' down in the local pond. But if you want a reason why women nag look no further than the size difference between them and men. What else can a woman do? If men don't want to change course, then trying to wrest the tiller out of their hand will merely end in sprains and bruises. There are only two things to be done: either let them have their way or mount a verbal campaign, in the hope that they will be worn down in time.

WHATEVER WOMEN DO THEY MUST DO TWICE AS WELL AS MEN TO BE THOUGHT HALF AS GOOD. LUCKILY, THIS IS NOT DIFFICULT.

(Charlotte Whitton)

There is another fall-out from male size – men not only dominate women, they also dominate the reporting of women. Male dominance in publishing has skewed the story of history, including the history of scientific discovery. Science history is His Story. The discoveries of women are often ignored or even stolen.

Cecilia Payne-Gaposchkin studied the spectrum of the sun in the 1920s and came to the conclusion that it must be made mainly of helium and hydrogen, rather than iron, the then current theory. If she had been a man the findings would have been published with much fanfare straight away. But the patronizing nature of the male scientists that surrounded her persuaded her to water down her findings. Princeton astronomer Henry Norris Russell wrote to her

that 'it is clearly impossible that hydrogen should be a million times more abundant than the metals'. He later discovered that she was right – and took credit for the discovery himself.

Slowly women scientists are being exhumed, like skeletons from a war grave, with mutterings of male remorse. Ada Lovelace, Cecilia Payne-Gaposchkin, Hypatia of Alexandria, Émilie du Châtele, to name but a few. Sometimes the old adage that 'behind every great man stands a great woman' should be rewritten; 'in front of every great woman stands a great big man'.

ON ONE ISSUE, AT LEAST, BOTH WOMEN AND MEN AGREE – THEY BOTH DISTRUST WOMEN.

(H. L. Mencken)

Another splendid Murphy; it sounds so wonderfully, resonantly true, yet it remains equally true if inverted.

BOTH MEN AND WOMEN DISTRUST MEN.

The last few pages have been written with the help of my difference engine. But stark differences barely exist, and certainly not for anyone I know: all people show some qualities you could call typical of their sex and some others you could say are exceptional. What a shame that, when there are so many caring dads and so many cold mums, so many socially brilliant men and wonderful woman managers, good women drivers and lousy male map-readers, that the differences between them have to be so stressed in mythology. Men will be for ever 'frogs, snails and puppy-dog tails', and women 'sugar and spice and all things nice', as in the nursery rhyme. This is one 'gulf war' which will never end.

NOBODY WILL EVER WIN THE BATTLE OF THE SEXES. THERE'S JUST TOO MUCH FRATERNIZING WITH THE ENEMY.

(Henry Kissinger)

COURTING DISASTER

The opposite sex – both male and female – is a riddle wrapped in a mystery, inside an enigma. Working out how they function is a tough enough task at the best of times, but when they are out searching for a boyfriend or girlfriend they put on a special act which only adds to the confusion – an act which bears comparison with the most elaborate seducer in the animal kingdom: the bower bird.

The bower bird

The bower bird is the master-builder of New Guinea. He not only performs a mating dance, as most other birds do, he also constructs his own extraordinary stage setting to perform it in. He builds his structure on the jungle floor. It may be a wide garden or a tall tower, carefully woven from grass and twigs, sometimes 3 metres (9 ft) high. The bower will be festooned with flowers, butterfly wings, anything colourful. The colour scheme is tastefully arranged, with perhaps red objects laid out in a pattern, while blue things are piled on one side. Another bower bird may only use yellow as a colour scheme. They're very fussy, very individual, and beautiful by any standards. (When Westerners first encountered them they thought they had been built by the natives.) All this from a creature no bigger than a pigeon, with a brain one thousandth the size of our own.

When a female bower bird hops by, she scrutinizes the architecture and examines the fixtures and fittings. While she's doing this he will be putting on a theatrical display, perhaps hiding behind his artful fencing, coyly waving one of his treasures at her, or strutting back and forth with his chest puffed out and his neck feathers erect. If she is impressed enough by his stuff and his strutting, they disappear together into the bushes to consummate, and she immediately sets about building a more modest nest of her own, laying and

rearing the brood, while he sets about seducing the next female. He takes no interest in child-rearing, being intent upon mating with as many females as possible.

FASHION IS WHAT YOU ADOPT WHEN YOU DON'T KNOW WHO YOU ARE.

(Quentin Crisp)

Are you a bower bird?

Is there not a parallel here? Your room or flat is like a bower bird's – laid out in a special way. You have spent many hours perfecting it, choosing the furniture, picking the décor, even down to the detail of whether there should be a matt, gloss or silk finish to the paint. Although the purpose of your flat is not entirely seduction, with that final flurry of the evening, arranging the flowers and candles, plumping the cushions and hiding the socks, your 'bower' is as beautiful as you can make it.

Out in the clubs and bars everyone, like a bower bird, has festooned their body with decorations. Their hair has been carefully arrayed (and if it looks carelessly tossed, you can be sure it was carefully carelessly tossed). A lot of thought has gone into the colour and style of clothes. You will be on display, so your plumage needs to 'send out the right signal'. Does your bum look big in this? Are the jeans casually ripped in exactly the right place? Added make-up, a suntan, jewellery, piercings, tattoos and fragrance complete the costume.

Faced with this elaborate display, the question is: what is it hiding? What is behind the mascara, beneath the padded shoulders? If we dig a little will we find the considerate, gentle human being we need? It is more important for humans to find the true person because humans do differ from bower birds in that last detail described above: the bower bird male is committed to mating with as many females as possible, while humans – as a rule at least – are searching for one long-term partner. Among the qualities necessary for a happy life together, skilful deployment of make-up and fragrance are less important than intelligence, commitment, respect and many other more dowdy qualities, none of which are on show today.

How will you ever find Mr Right or Miss Perfect?

WHEN PEOPLE ARE FREE TO DO AS THEY PLEASE, THEY USUALLY IMITATE EACH OTHER.

(Eric Hoffer)

Mimicry

The display we put on owes much to our special feature, the brain. Animals with small brains, like insects, use fixed actions in any given situation, whereas humans can adapt their behaviour to suit the circumstance. Therefore, small-brainers don't do any training. They already know exactly what they will do in all circumstances. Humans (and bower birds) have to programme their brain before they can seriously use it. The way they download information is through 'mimicry', copying those around them using their mirror neurons (see pp. 4, 107). In this way they absorb everything, big and small. Big things for humans include techniques of hunting and team-work, language, family values, morals and ethics. Small things include social skills, dialect, catch-phrases, dance styles and fashion.

Small-brainers and big-brainers alike are apt to look absurd under special circumstances: the small-brainer because of how much they can't modify their behaviour; the big-brainer because of how much they can. A small-brainer like a fly keeps bashing its head against a windowpane because it can't adapt. Big-brainers can be embarrassed by how much they were able to adapt, how much they slavishly followed the trends. Older big-brainers will look at pictures of themselves aged eighteen and say 'Did I really wear my hair like *that*?'

TO BE NATURAL IS SUCH A VERY DIFFICULT POSE TO KEEP UP.

(Oscar Wilde)

There is no such thing as natural

In public, everything about you is an act, bought, begged or borrowed from the surrounding world. Or stolen. (Bower birds, by the way, are consummate thieves. Only half their time is spent creating their own wonders, the other half is taken up in stealing from their neighbour. They know they won't find their neighbour at home, because *he* is out stealing from his neighbour on the other side.)

Back in your home town everyone is indulging in their own kind of robbery, of a perfectly legitimate type – style theft. What we really covet from our neighbour is not their hi-fi or car but their panache, their accent, attitude or mannerisms. We use mirror neurons to make a copy, almost without thinking.

As you have begun to put yourself on display to the opposite sex in recent months, you have been studying your friends and eyeing up a range of behaviours which seem promising. A particular phrase sounds good? Use it. A good smile, cobbled together from bits of George Clooney and pieces of Robbie Williams? Slap it on! You have also picked up over several years the correct way to arrange your legs when sitting down (real ladies keep them together), how to shake hands (not too firm, not too soft), how to stick out the little finger when drinking tea . . . a million little social graces.

'KNOW THYSELF'? IF I KNEW MYSELF, I'D RUN AWAY.

(Johann Wolfgang von Goethe)

Are there any bits of you that aren't an act?

Tragically, yes! Your body language speaks louder than all the frills. Are you being affirmative, open and friendly or negative, closed and frightened? We can tell by looking at you, and so could a passing chimp; this is an instinctive behaviour which dates back to your simian ancestry.

Some of your body language goes back to an even earlier ancestor and is shared by the goldfish. When you hear a disgusting story you may shake your head and turn away from the teller in exactly the same way as a goldfish turns its head away from pungent smells in the water.

Some parents think it is so vital to stifle these instinctive signals and replace them with more socially acceptable ones that they send their offspring to finishing school, where they will learn no academic subjects but 'Modern Manners, Social Skills and Personal Presentation'. Armed with the stylistic façade, they will be able to act for all the world as if they know what they're talking about, without their body language giving the game away.

PLAIN WOMEN KNOW MORE ABOUT MEN THAN BEAUTIFUL ONES DO.

(Katharine Hepburn)

Male courtship displays

Men, like bower birds, put on a special burlesque for the one they lust after, and it can be quite frightening. Katharine Hepburn was a famous Hollywood star from 1931 to 1994, and was loved from afar by many men. She found it disconcerting at times when total strangers (who had fallen in love with her in a cinema somewhere) would turn into crazies in her company, waving their arms, cracking loud jokes, giggling, bursting into song in the middle of the street to try and impress her. On one occasion, a trip across a harbour on a motor launch turned nightmarish when the ferryman revved up to full speed and near-crashed into the opposite harbour wall as a demonstration of his derring-do. These male acts, Ms Hepburn realized, were not the real world; they were weird dances, which men performed whenever she was around, then dropped when she had gone. Beautiful women have no idea what life on earth is really like. They never meet men, only clowns. They only get the glitz, while plain women get the grit.

Katharine Hepburn herself put on no show. Confident of her looks, she was utterly down to earth off-set (wearing *trousers*, my dear!), to the despair of the studio publicity agents and the mortification of any man who put on airs around her.

TO FIND OUT A GIRL'S FAULTS, PRAISE HER TO HER GIRLFRIENDS.

(Benjamin Franklin)

How to see through the act

The girl you have just been talking to, Benjamin, was very sweet and seemed to like you. She put on a great show – smiling, agreeing and laughing at your jokes. But if you want to take the relationship further you need to find out who she really is because, to be perfectly honest, you never met *her* while you were talking with her. You met a number of her friends, her parents and an actress she once admired. These were significant people in her life. She studied and copied them. All were fleeced for useful mannerisms which she now displays for your delight. Her act is a fabrication.

When she's among her friends she is not performing, so they know her true self, the one she hides. So one thing you could do is praise her to her friends. That would raise their hackles high enough for them to tell you about the real her.

Alternatively you could invite her to share some interesting times in your company. Remember that plan you had to fly a kite through a thunderstorm to see what the lightning did to it? Invite her along. That way you'll find out things about her she hoped to keep secret for a lot longer, like her hatred of getting wet, and her extensive range of swear-words.

THE FIRST TIME YOU BUY A HOUSE YOU SEE HOW PRETTY THE PAINT IS AND BUY IT. THE SECOND TIME YOU LOOK TO SEE IF THE BASEMENT HAS TERMITES. IT'S THE SAME WITH MEN.

(Lupe Velez)

Are men any good in the long run?

So Adonis has that special smile, does he? The hilarious jokes and witty stories? The poetry, the stylish clothes, hairstyle, medallion? The extensive knowledge of fine wines? What more could you want in a man?

Wait until Adonis tries to make a cup of tea and has to ask you for the recipe. Oh, the disappointment when the exquisitely honed and toned body can't hold a tin-opener the right way up. So you'll have to do all the cooking and, so it turns out, the washing up afterwards. Still, he looks gorgeous lying on the sofa with a glass of Rioja between his fingers, even if

BRAIN THE SIZE OF A PEA

he seems to have only three hilarious jokes, which he tells in rotation. But when you find that his knowledge of fine wines is not just theoretical but has a disturbingly practical side, then maybe it's time to call it a day.

Truth is, Adonis hasn't designed his act for a long-term relationship. He only has short liaisons. He is more like a bower bird than he ought to be, setting out his arena with enough temptation to attract a passing female, dallying with them for a while, then pressing on to the next.

BRAINS ARE AN ASSET, IF YOU HIDE THEM.

(Mae West)

Are women allowed to be intelligent?

You would have thought that in our complex modern world intelligence in women would be a good thing. And yet, some men don't like it. Here the ancient ape and the modern man come into conflict. Ape-men ruled by virtue of their larger size. In the intellectual arena, though, men don't have the same advantage. Girls nowadays are getting the same or higher grades than boys right across the curriculum. But boys still do better than girls in sport, and when they feel like it they can win a fight with a girl. Which means boys get their way.

Mae West's advice to women is to be as clever as they know they are, but pretend not to be, to avoid a fight. Faking it is quite hard, but most women can do it. And they do do it, more often than men would like to believe. So in arguments with her over-large man a woman may concede. But perhaps this is not so soft as it seems.

He wants to go to Milan for a holiday. She doesn't want the hassle. Wouldn't Blackpool be easier? He puts his foot down. She 'bends like a reed'. Over the next couple of days the conversations seem to come round to global warming quite a lot. He becomes quite agitated about waste of precious resources. She finds out the amount of fuel consumed by the plane to Milan, and tells him. Soon they've booked a week at the Grand Metropole, Princess Parade, Blackpool.

MEN DON'T MAKE PASSES AT FEMALE SMART-ASSES.

(Lettie Gottin Pogrebin)

Playing the dumb blonde?

Women learn to play the gentle game very early on. Since childhood they have been buffeted by testosterone-charged lads, and they know how hard it is to be an immovable object when faced with the irresistible force of male certainty. They have had a lifetime to learn all the acting skills necessary to stay in one piece. When men search in the Lonely Hearts pages for women with 'GSOH', what they don't desire is wiseacres or comediennes. That's not what a Good Sense Of Humour means. 'GSOH' means 'will laugh uproariously at *his* jokes'. Allegedly, what men seek is a dumb blonde.

Dolly Parton, the American Country singer has a tremendous dumb blonde act. Everything about her says sweet and gullible, will laugh at everyone else's jokes and won't dare to advance one of her own. But she wouldn't be where she is if she were really that dim. Truth is, there's a powerful intellect sitting just behind the fluff. Let her have the last word:

> I'm not offended by all the dumb blonde jokes because I know I'm not dumb… and I also know that I'm not blonde.

BEAUTY IS SKIN DEEP; UGLY GOES RIGHT TO THE BONE.

Speed-dating

Some of the attributes we call beauty are not merely a matter of personal taste, but have practical aspects: a beautiful skin, because a smooth-looking skin is a clue to a healthy body and effective immune system; symmetry of face and figure, because asymmetry might indicate unwanted genetic flaws; the bower bird's display gives an instant cross-section of his technical skills, energy, etc. Sometimes humans have just as short a time to impress – witness the annual Geerewol festival of the Wodaabe.

Wodaabe males at the annual Geerewol festival.

The Wodaabe are a proud nomadic people who are scattered across the sub-Saharan Sahel region of Niger, West Africa. Their grand gatherings, or Geerewol, are an opportunity – in fact, the only opportunity – for the women to pick a husband. Height, clear skin, white teeth and sparkling eyes are considered most desirable in their men. But these people are nomadic – they'll soon be splitting off again across the desert. So the hopeful men have developed a dance in which to rapidly show off all these points of beauty. They stand in front of the girls on tip-toes to gain height, rolling their eyes to show off how white they are, grinning broadly to show off their teeth all the while. The Wodaabe girls must choose quickly on the basis of this evidence alone.

IF NATURE HAD INTENDED OUR SKELETONS TO BE VISIBLE IT WOULD HAVE PUT THEM ON THE OUTSIDE OF OUR BODIES.

(Elmer Rice)

How thin is thin enough?

Slim figures are considered beautiful in the West. But they were not always thought of in this way. Classical paintings of Venus, goddess of love, often depict a quite stout beauty, and for good reason. In earlier times, when food was short, spare fat reserves were useful. Child-bearing is demanding on the mother's bodily resources, so plumpness was an asset. Rubens's *The Judgement of Paris* (c. 1632) shows three girls who were considered beautiful in their time, but they wouldn't make the glamour mags today. In fact, many Asian and African cultures look at the modern Western world's fashion shows with slight horror – super-models look half-starved to a Tahitian.

Men in the past also used to be more attractive if they were fat. Corpulence was a sign of wealth. Not any more; today, obesity is associated with rich food but poor diet.

Rubens's *The Judgement of Paris* (c. 1632)

TELL ME, TELL ME, TELL ME WHY I WANT TO KNOW THE FACT: WHY ALL THE BLACK PEOPLE WANT TO GO WHITE AND THE WHITE PEOPLE WANT TO GO BLACK.

(Jeremy Taylor)

To tan or not to tan

Fashion in skin colour has been a roller-coaster over the centuries. In Europe up until the twentieth century, tanned skin was ugly, a sign of a life lived in the fields. To emphasize their aristocratic pretensions, ladies at court would cover themselves up because white flesh was considered beautiful, the mark of a princess (hence Snow White). Nowadays the exact reverse holds: white skin denotes a life of office drudgery, while a tanned skin speaks of hours spent relaxing in the sun, the prerogative of the idle rich. In South-East Asia, however, pale skin looks European and is desired so much by the women that face-whitening soap is on sale in shops everywhere. If regularly used, it will remove the very tan which Europeans spend so long trying to cultivate. Meanwhile, in Europe, men and women who toil indoors can have a tan sprayed on to make it look as if they have nothing better to do than jet to and from the Bahamas. The treatment takes ten minutes, so it can be easily slotted into the office schedule.

LOVE IS AN IRRESISTIBLE DESIRE TO BE IRRESISTIBLY DESIRED.

(Robert Frost)

Finessing the act

Here is the catch: if a girl wants to be desired, there is no problem. She can dress attractively and hit the town. But there may be someone out there who will irresistibly desire her just a bit too irresistibly. Unwelcome advances from men are always a danger when you put yourself about.

How can a girl put on an act to attract a male, yet keep all the other men at bay until the right one comes along? You have to be able to simultaneously bring them on and push them back, like a peculiar fisherman's baited hook, which must try to attract all fish but be able to shake off the unwanted ones. It is a very difficult balancing act. An effective performance will radiate honesty, empathy and affection towards all males you encounter. The men will be at your feet. But they must not overstep the mark. At the same time as you give off the oh-so-natural, carefree image on the surface, you must monitor acutely the effect you are having. There are invisible rules of flirtation: no suggestive comments, no touching. Any transgression of the rules by any male and the guillotine will come down on the conversation. You will signal that the interview is over and he is no longer welcome. If you're lucky, he will notice.

NICE ASSESSMENT

Life is like a jigsaw with a lot of pieces missing. You have to fill in the spaces with your imagination. Fortunately the brain has the necessary mechanisms to do this. Unfortunately the mechanisms are a little ropey.

Fortunately this gives us the chance to study the psychology of perception under extreme conditions (lust).

Unfortunately we won't be any more competent as a result of the study.

NEVER GET TOO EXCITED BY WHAT THEY LOOK LIKE FROM BEHIND.

Guessing game

Psychologists have isolated three mechanisms for analyzing the world:

Attention focusing: you only focus on a few features and ignore the rest – you only use a few 'pieces of the jigsaw'.

When you find yourself fancying someone from behind, the pieces of jigsaw are the back views of the legs, buttocks, shoulders, hair.

Cognitive miserliness: you come to the easiest conclusion you can about what you see. In this case, back view nice, therefore front view nice.

Naive science: you make a connection between what you see in order to tell a story, slipping in some extra jigsaw pieces of your own if you have to. In this case you have seen what you guess is a very attractive person, so you imagine you and he/she would hit it off really well if only you could get to know her or him better.

I will call the terrible trio **Simple** thinking, **Illogical** thinking and **Naive** thinking – or S.I.N. for short.

SEX APPEAL IS 50 PER CENT WHAT YOU'VE GOT AND 50 PER CENT WHAT PEOPLE THINK YOU'VE GOT.

Application of S.I.N.

S.I.N. is easily applied to clothing, where if you reveal 50 per cent of your body but conceal 50 per cent, S.I.N. fills in the missing 50 per cent.

The most sensual images of men and women work not because they are naked, but because they are nearly so. It is strange that people seem to want the opposite sex nude but prefer the sight of them half-clothed. It is called 'revealing clothing', which of course is not the right word; clothes are by definition concealing. What is being revealed is the imagination of the onlooker.

The 50/50 proportions change when people are deprived of the opposite sex for some length of time – a month at sea perhaps. Now sex appeal need only be 10 per cent what you've got. The poor soul in front of you is working their imagination at a valve-bursting 90 per cent.

KEEP QUIET AND PEOPLE WILL THINK YOU A PHILOSOPHER.

Less is More

Research suggests that over 50 per cent of your character is deduced from your body language, about 30 per cent from your style of speaking, and less than 10 per cent from what you actually say. So keep mute. Open your mouth and you'll ruin the effect.

You might like to work on your body language, since it accounts for 50 per cent of your charm. On the up side, there are many books on the subject nowadays. On the down side, if you try to carry them all home, your body language for the following few weeks will say 'cripple'.

For the time being, if you have to join in conversation, try to talk as little as possible. Give them just a few bits of 'jigsaw' and watch them invent the rest of the picture, using S.I.N. to help them.

BEFORE YOU FIND YOUR HANDSOME PRINCE, YOU'VE GOT TO KISS A LOT OF FROGS.

The power of S.I.N.

This Murphy's Law is disingenuous. You do have to kiss a lot of frogs, certainly, but they don't seem like frogs when you decide to kiss them, do they? They seem like princes. Only as your lips meet does the prince turn into an amphibian.

How can a frog look like a prince? Because of S.I.N., which so easily builds a fairy-tale romance between you.

He is a prince. He IS. Perhaps a little on the short side, but a lot of princes are short. Yours can still be a deep, fulfilling relationship. So what if he has wide feet, and spends a lot of time in the swimming pool, and is green. Yours is a love big enough to transcend the species barrier.

Then the kiss, the wet, cold kiss — and reality bites. Another disappointment. As you leave, shaking your head in disbelief that you were taken in by a frog yet again, you promise never to let that recur. From now on you will be careful.

After a week, though, you are so desperate for love you ask the fridge out on a date.

IT IS AMAZING HOW COMPLETE IS THE DELUSION THAT BEAUTY IS GOODNESS.

(Leo Tolstoy)

The 'pretty' pitfall

Why do we fall for pretty people? Is it just S.I.N., our Simple minds only looking at the outward appearance, our Illogical thinking assuming the best, our Naive narrative telling the sweetest story? Fairy tales we are told as children are populated by 'handsomes' and 'beautifuls' who are good, being set upon by 'uglys' who are evil. To simplify things further, anyone over the age of twenty-five is ancient, therefore definitely ugly and probably evil to boot. Standards are being set at an early age, it seems.

We have seen the biological reason to be more attracted to faces that have good skin and hair tone and are symmetrical (see p. 53), but, as Tolstoy points out, the delusion that beauty = goodness is almost total. A useful guiding principle has become an irrefutable law.

But there is another factor, which is covered on p.99. When we decide we love someone, they do indeed become beautiful. Our perception of them changes. Simple, illogical and naive as we are, we grasp the 50 per cent that's on offer and add a generous 50 per cent of our own.

BRAINS × GOOD LOOKS × AVAILABILITY = 0

The science of the perfect partner

Statisticians have tracked down many interesting data that suggest a predictable way to find the perfect match: people tend to choose partners from the same ethnic background; they tend to be the same ages, of the same religion, similar socio-economic stratum, share the same political views, have similar interests, have similar IQs, and live in the same area. No surprises there. It narrows the field of possible partners down to a couple of thousand. But there are more surprising overlaps. According to the statistics, they tend to have similar wrist sizes, ear lobe sizes, breadth of nose, middle-finger length and inter-occular distance (between the eyes), even lung capacity!

So statisticians have the answer. All we need to do is post our dimensions up on the web and wait for someone with a matching set to pop along. Bingo! No more need for love. It's all sorted with the click of a mouse.

Statisticians need to get out more.

POWER IS THE ULTIMATE APHRODISIAC.
(Henry Kissinger)

The power of power

Henry Kissinger certainly had to have something going for him other than his looks. Indeed the string of unattractive politicians who manage to seduce their secretaries must give us pause for thought. The evolutionary psychologist will point knowingly at the protective/nurturing value of the power and wealth such people command and say 'told you so'. Throughout the animal kingdom, power and wealth means territory and food for the offspring; the power to establish and maintain a territory is vital, whether

it is the river-bed nest guarded zealously by the stickleback or the territory ranged by the chimp, or come to that the hegemony of the Austro-Hungarian Empire.

Geoffrey Miller, in his book *The Mating Mind: How Sexual Choice Shaped the Evolution of Human Nature*, sees the displays that politicians mount in Parliament as little more than sexual come-ons on a level with the peacock flashing his tail. As with all courtship rituals, one can recognize them by certain biological criteria. 'They are expensive to produce and hard to maintain, they have survival costs but reproductive benefits, they are loud, bright, rhythmic, complex and creative to stimulate the senses, they occur more often after reproductive maturity, more often during the breeding season . . .'

MY PROBLEM LIES IN RECONCILING MY GROSS HABITS WITH MY NET INCOME.

(Errol Flynn)

What we are searching for

Researchers in every country, whether rich or poor, discover to nobody's great surprise that girls find wealth, or the potential to gain it, attractive. The reasons are not hard to see. They are the same as the bower bird's attraction to the best-decorated nest or the sea-cow's attraction to the fattest male. If babies are to be cared for, food and nesting space will be needed. The man with the richest façade is most likely to provide that.

Can you imagine that a girl who is gazing deep into your eyes is actually looking right through you to your last three years' bank statements? If she's level-headed and considering you as a partner she needs to do that.

The problem lies with that phrase: 'If she's level-headed . . .' Who, aside from Mr Spock, is level-headed? As we will soon discover, our instincts and our emotions are in constant collision with good sense and decorum. Level heads go into a steep dive when they fall in love . . .

**IF YOU FEEL ROMANTIC, LADDY,
LET ME WARN YOU RIGHT FROM THE START
THAT MY HEART BELONGS TO DADDY
AND MY DADDY BELONGS TO MY HEART.**

(Cole Porter)

Family values

Another set of judgements you make when picking the right partner take you back to your childhood. Your parents, the first love objects in your life, influence your choice. Men like girlfriends who remind them of Mum, girls are searching for Dad.

An experiment quoted in Patrick Bateson's book *Mate Choice* involved rearing Japanese quails, which come in two colours, white or brown. Some quail eggs were swapped, so that one white quail was reared by brown parents, with brown siblings, while the white family found itself with one brown quail offspring. On reaching maturity, the odd coloured quails tended to mate more readily with the 'wrong' coloured quails. They were happier with the colour they had been brought up amongst. You too, it seems, enjoy the company of your family enough to seek something similar in a partner.

YOU SHOULD MAKE A POINT OF TRYING EVERY EXPERIENCE ONCE, EXCEPTING INCEST AND FOLK-DANCING.

(Sir Arnold Bax)

Incest

There is one place where one can find people who are like one in many ways, and that is right here at home. Why don't we marry into our own family and save time? They are readily available, they share lots of our traits, and they know our little ways.

The reason why that would be a disaster is to do with our genes. The process of making babies which humans and most animals employ – sexual reproduction – means that we carry two sets of genes, one from our mother, one from our father. If Arnold's parents are actually brother and sister both sets of genes will be similar. If there is a flaw in their genes, Arnold is doubly likely to inherit it, and will very likely suffer as a result.

Cystic fibrosis is caused by a mutation in a gene called the 'cystic fibrosis transmembrane conductance regulator' (CFTR). We get the CFTR gene from both parents (so we have two CFTRs), and provided just one of them is OK, we are OK. Our parents could be carriers, they might have one mutant gene, but still not have the disease, because the other CFTR gene functions properly.

If they each pass a mutant gene to Arnold, he will have two faulty CFTRs and will suffer from the disease. This happens often enough in the world – one in twenty-five of us carry the gene – but in incest the likelihood of the child suffering the disease is much higher. That's why incest is a bad idea. The argument against folk-dancing is self-evident.

FAMILIARITY BREEDS CONTEMPT.

Why incest doesn't happen

In spite of the logical argument against incest, one would expect the easiness of it to overcome most objections. Why is there so little of it? There are two reasons. Firstly, there is no romance.

In 1971, Joseph Shepher studied 2,769 children in an Israeli kibbutz. They had all been born in the kibbutz, and following kibbutz tradition they were removed from special contact with their parents and reared with others of the same age in community-run nurseries where they played, ate, slept and were educated together. Adults were supposed to think of all the kibbutz children as joint social property and were discouraged from developing particularly close relationships with their own offspring. When they came to be of marrying age, all but thirteen looked for partners outside the kibbutz. Even though there was no danger of incest for the vast majority of them they could not think of their 'brothers and sisters' as possible marriage fodder. Familiarity bred, if not contempt, then indifference.

The second reason why incest is rare is discussed in the section on hormones, on pp. 90–1; we can smell when we are attracted to the wrong person. Their genetic type is being advertised through the emission, in their sweat, of tiny signal molecules, pheromones, which tell us unconsciously if their genes are the right ones for us.

I BELIEVE IN GETTING INTO HOT WATER; IT KEEPS YOU CLEAN.

(G.K. Chesterton)

The handicap principle

Evolutionary psychologists have to explain some pretty strange types of behaviour, for instance risk-taking, boozing or drug abuse. Men do these things and think they are more like real men for it, and many women are attracted to it. But does it confer an evolutionary advantage? The kindly scientists have set themselves up to search for a perfectly rational explanation for what seems pretty irrational to most of us.

Possibly evolutionary biologist Amotz Zahavi got it right. The 'handicap principle' he first proposed in 1975 starts by trying to explain the inexplicably useless peacock's tail, which looks stylish, but gets in the way of a quick escape when there's a predator nearby. The peahens, looking for a male who can escape being eaten before they have raised their brood, should shun any male with such an encumbrance. In other words, evolution should have seen to it that the peacock's tail disappeared. But it persists, to the delight of peahens and the perplexity of ethologists. According to Zahavi, what the peacock's tail is saying is 'look at me, I have this gigantic impediment stuck to my backside, yet I am still able to prance, preen and be useful. I must be mega-fit!' Extending the argument, that would explain binge-drinking. The bloke says, 'Look at me, I get smashed every weekend, yet I can still stagger in to work on a Monday and handle heavy machinery. Will you marry me?' Well, just because an argument is far-fetched, it doesn't mean it's wrong. Duelling scars were much sought after in the days of the sword. Nowadays bullet wounds are displayed with pride. A leg in plaster from a skiing accident advertises bravery, rather than lack of skill at skiing. There is something about a broken nose . . .

SLITHERY SLOPES

So far we have held back from the precipice. In a rather innocent way we have looked fairly coolly at the ways you relate to others, whether family friends or the opposite sex, and at the stately courtship dance you perform with them. Now it is time to set off down the slope from which there is no return. At the top of the slope sits lust. At the bottom lie broken hearts. Wriggle as you might, if you touch the one you will end up among the other. The slippery slope is lubricated with hormones.

LOVE IS ONLY A DIRTY TRICK PLAYED ON US TO ACHIEVE CONTINUATION OF THE SPECIES.

(W. Somerset Maugham)

Hormones are the chemicals which rule the limbic system, right in the centre of the most primitive part of the brain.

Hormones were around in one shape or another 3,000 million years ago, controlling the behaviour of the bacteria, which would eventually evolve into man (see p.173). On the other hand, human intelligence is a much more recent invention; nerves began to appear, in jellyfish, only about six hundred million years ago. However much the nervous system evolved since then it has never really been able to influence the more basic urges of the hormones. Indeed, the nervous system evolved to make the hormones more efficient, not the other way around. Any smoker will tell you how much the chemical urges dominate the grey matter's musings. The intellect can be full of any amount of convincing evidence about the bad effects of smoking, but the urge to smoke will win out in the end. When it comes to sex, the same applies. Hormones rule.

THERE IS NO DIFFERENCE BETWEEN A WISE MAN AND A FOOL WHEN THEY FALL IN LOVE.

Hormones

The hormones involved with the loving feelings are not to be argued with. They will turn you upside down and shake you until your teeth rattle, and are decidedly unavailable to reasoned argument (which the wise man might use to defend himself). Your needle-sharp intellect will be dissolved by the potent chemicals which are oozing from your limbic system.

You will become excited because adrenaline will have been squeezed out of your adrenal gland, next to your kidneys. You will desire sex suddenly, since testosterone has popped out from your testicles or your ovaries (p.93). You will feel euphoric because phenylethylamine (PEA) appeared in your bloodstream (p.94). Your feeling of attachment will be due to the emergence of vasopressin (p.103), deep joy will be down to oxytocin (p.103), and most particularly, oh wise sage, there is a cataclysmic loss of wisdom, caused by a lowered level of serotonin (p.99).

The problem the wise man has is that he has further to fall. A fool is a fool; a wise man has put a lot of effort into not being foolish. How embarrassing is that!

DO YOU BELIEVE IN LOVE AT FIRST SIGHT, OR DO I HAVE TO WALK PAST YOU AGAIN?

The urge to love

Love At First Sight is the duck-billed platypus of the mind: it's totally preposterous, but undeniably there. Scientists have got to find an explanation for LAFS.

The first LAFS can happen close to the onset of puberty. You might be only thirteen, but already there's a pop star on your wall. This is LAFS: you are infatuated by someone you've never even met. Your 'first sight' was on *Top of the Pops*, and you adored them instantly.

Some time later the same thing happens, but this time with someone real, and right there in front of you. This is the more dangerous form of the condition. So it may help to know what's going on inside you as you stand there gawping.

The first thing we learn from studying LAFS is that we are built for love. We are baby-making machines, and we come from a long line of baby-making machines, stretching back a very long time. Since the first DNA molecule first split in two 3.5 billion years ago, evolution has only happened to those who made the next generation, which would make the next generation, and so on. There was very little room for playing hard to get, dating or any of that stuff; only the fast movers made it through to the next round.

When Love At First Sight happens to you, you know you are ready to take evolution forward once again.

THE ONLY TRUE LOVE IS LOVE AT FIRST SIGHT; SECOND SIGHT DISPELS IT.

(Israel Zangwill)

Why there is no alternative

Why that particular person is so dazzlingly wonderful, while the other people in the room – equally interesting in their own ways – seem so colourless, has been the subject of considerable research.

First off, this is not a divine spark. That is not an angel in front of you, even though it shimmers like one. You were not destined to meet. You were not made for each other. The entire cosmos was not constructed and directed towards this exact moment.

It does feel like that, though, doesn't it? And there's a good psychological reason why.

Your first reaction was from your hormones. It is your limbic system and its primitive chemicals which are in the driving seat. Your cerebral cortex came along later and tried to make some sense of the disorder. In other words, you don't say 'There is a person in front of me who has a clear skin, symmetrical eyes, excellent poise and the same inter-occular distance as me, therefore I had better feel loving emotions.' You say 'Grief, my pants are on fire! My heart is pounding! I've gone pink all over! How am I going to interpret this emotion? Well, that must be a divine angel I'm looking at; that's the only logical explanation!!' Lust is the first response; the second one, if you manage to hold on long enough, is a cooler appraisal.

A HEN IS ONLY AN EGG'S WAY OF MAKING ANOTHER EGG.

(Samuel Butler)

How to procreate

There are many different ways of creating the next generation. Some animals do it by splurging eggs and semen all over the place and crossing their fingers (or fins, since it's herring I'm thinking of here). Others, like us, are more fastidious, making babies slowly, one at a time, and carefully looking after each one. For years.

Now, when you experience the heart-pounding, hot-flushing, stammering, slightly dribbling embarrassment which is LAFS, what your body is telling you to do is have sex with the beloved absolutely right here and right now. But you don't. If you were a herring you would, but you are a human and we don't splurge, we take our time. A most elaborate courtship ritual is about to take place, which will take weeks or months, perhaps years.

NOTICE

The following 20 pages do not reflect the views of management

There is a sort of shorthand in the Murphy's Laws that follow. 'Men prefer . . .' and 'Women always go for . . .' are hopeless generalizations (see p. 21). Remarks like that crop up in boorishly sexist gossip and, like all sexist remarks, they are absolutely true on average, and absolutely not true for the individual in front of you. However, the following pages are full of them. I apologize.

IT UPSETS WOMEN TO BE, OR NOT TO BE, STARED AT HUNGRILY.

(Mignon McLaughlin)

A tale of two cities

A young Spanish woman walks down a street in Edinburgh. On the way she passes several groups of young men, on building sites, in cafes, loitering on street corners. None of them stare, call out or whistle. At the end of her walk she is ready to cry. What, she wonders, is wrong with her? Is she really that unattractive?

A British woman walks down a similar street in Seville. By the end she is livid. These Spanish men, she mutters, are all apes.

IT IS BETTER TO BE LOOKED OVER THAN OVERLOOKED.

How much do we desire attention?

Spanish women have been brought up to expect the attention, and understand that the sexual undertone is not threatening. (In spite of appearances, rapes in Spain run at a quarter the level of Britain.) British women don't expect all that attention in public, and feel threatened.

What would happen if the roles were reversed? When the women wear the trousers it is the men who are looked over. Women-only businesses are scary places for a messenger boy to deliver parcels to. Isolated from his mates and surrounded by the enemy, he is not so brash as he would be down the pub. Groups of women are capable of pretty humiliating (sexist, even) behaviour towards men. In Britain, Friday nights offer a chance to see predatory gangs of drunken women roaming the city centres, in every way like a bunch of 'lads'. Put these ladettes in overalls and set them to work on a Spanish building site and they would be whistling at the men in the street below all right, and the men would be a little bit indignant and a little bit pleased. Nobody, whether a man or a woman, whether Scottish, Arabic or Icelandic, wants to be ignored entirely.

IF YOU GET THEM BY THE BALLS, THEIR HEARTS AND MINDS WILL FOLLOW.

(President Lyndon B. Johnson)

Bottom-up thinking

During the Malay emergency in the 1950s, Harold Macmillan talked of 'winning the hearts and minds of the people' as his chief means of defusing the insurgents. Lyndon B. Johnson later added the 'balls' part as his rationale for escalating the Vietnam War in the 1960s. Johnson was referring to the fact that when argument isn't working, the threat of castration can be quite an effective way of winning the discussion.

My use of the saying is slightly different to President Johnson's — to point out the inverted thinking of the human brain. First we experience an emotion; secondly we work out what it means. In other words, we will trust our emotions before our rational thinking. In love talk, this means that once we've fallen in lust our other thoughts will obediently trail along behind; respect, admiration, trust, all act as bridesmaids to lust.

(This way we have of emoting first and thinking later can get us into a lot of trouble in other situations. What about anger — road rage and the like? We are told that when angry we should count to ten to allow rational, calming thoughts to rise. We should be taught that when we fall in love we should count to ten weeks likewise.)

LOVE UNLOCKS DOORS AND OPENS WINDOWS THAT WEREN'T EVEN THERE BEFORE.

(Mignon McLaughlin)

Pheromones

Practically the only thing that is known about pheromones is how to spell the word. Aside from that, all is ignorance. In the wild we know that signal odours are emitted by animals to attract mates, spread alarm, signal food, etc. But scientists are unhappy to think that our human pongs are good for anything but deodorizing.

But evidence is emerging – for instance about menstrual synchrony. It has been shown that female college room-mates tend to menstruate at the same time. Interestingly, this synchronization may be achieved solely by wiping underarm sweat from 'donor' women on to the upper lips of 'recipient' women, strongly suggesting that human pheromones may be contained in sweat and dispersed from the hair in our armpits. PET brain scans have shown that smelling an oestrogen-like compound produces increased blood flow in part of the hypothalamus in men, but not in women. Likewise, smelling an androgen related to testosterone produced increased blood flow in the same part of the hypothalamus in women, but not in men.

If you have felt an electric buzz when in the company of someone who fancies you, you should put it down to pheromones. Let's face up to the reality: underarm hair is an organ, not an embarrassment. The large surface area provided by the hairs disseminates odours more efficiently.

Shaving armpits is like applying a gag to a very important means of communication.

IT IS ABSURD TO DIVIDE PEOPLE INTO GOOD AND BAD. PEOPLE ARE EITHER CHARMING OR TEDIOUS.

(Oscar Wilde)

The importance of smell

What is charming, in our opinion, and what is tedious? Do we want a partner who is the same as us or who is different? Some say that they should be like us, and then they'll share the same beliefs and hobbies, laugh at the same jokes and be a generally perfect companion. Others say they should be opposites, fill the spaces we leave, and form, with us, a perfect combination. Well, the answer is quite surprising; it doesn't matter what your taste in fashion and music is, it probably all comes down to how you smell.

Smell is the most important of our senses. It is so important that the front part of the limbic system (the olfactory bulb) projects forward to just behind the nose so that smells can be assayed as quickly as possible.

More to the point in our search for a partner, smell may help to explain why the most unlikely people fall in love, and why the most likely pairings fail. The sorts of smell I'm on about here are nothing to do with perfumes or deodorants; it is a pheromone so subtle that you will not be aware of it. It is the smell of your immune system. Read on . . .

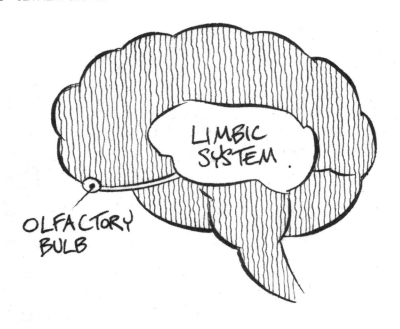

THE ONE YOU FANCY NEVER FANCIES YOU.

The major histocompatibility complex

She clearly likes you. You've enjoyed each other's company for weeks. She says you're the nicest guy . . . so where did it all go wrong?

Maybe it was your smell that was wrong. Not your pong, but the near-invisible smell of your immune system. This ability to unconsciously smell a person's immune system is the most primitive sense you have. Animals were sorting themselves out this way when they were still no more than Precambrian blobs. It is a vital defence against attack by parasites.

Your immune system is involved in killing off foreign invaders. How do your body's defenders know if the cell they've come across is part of the body or alien invader, friend or foe? The body's cells have identifying molecules, like a molecular barcode, on their surface. They are created by a part of your chromosomes called the Major Histocompatibility Complex (MHC). Aliens without the molecular code are attacked. If bugs could crack the code and disguise themselves as a legitimate part of the body they would be ignored by the immune system, and could go romping, infecting the body at will. So they are busily mutating. When a mutated code matches the body's own code the bearer will pass unchallenged through the body's defences. The body must keep ahead of the 'code-breakers' by mutating its own immune system. It is a constant race, which Matt Ridley, journalist and writer on genetics and human behaviour, likens to the Red Queen from Lewis Carroll's *Through the Looking Glass* – running like crazy in order to stay in the same place.

If animals have similar MHCs, whether they are Precambrian blobs or Camilla and Bob, the amount of gene-shuffling that can be done is limited and the possibility of the offspring being infected with disease is much greater. So, since the days of the flatworm, your particular brand of MHC has been advertised in your body odour and, unless hers is different from his, there's every chance that, for no reason that you can put your finger on, your love will just not blossom.

This has been confirmed by Swiss scientist Claus Wedekind and colleagues at the University of Berne. They asked a group of men to wear T-shirts until they were slightly whiffy, then some female students were asked to sniff them to see which they preferred. It turned out that the smells they preferred were for men with different MHC genes.

WE ALL WORRY ABOUT THE POPULATION EXPLOSION, BUT WE DON'T WORRY ABOUT IT AT THE RIGHT TIME.

(Arthur Hoppe)

Testosterone

After a delicious evening spent in social intercourse with the one you fancy, delving deeply in to questions of population control, what better way to round things off than by making babies? Once the passions are roused there's no holding back. The need for sex overrides any rational thoughts. Testosterone is the usual suspect for this sexual imperative. It has been called the hormone of desire, responsible for male aggression and insatiable sexual appetite, which sweeps aside any quibbles about the ifs and buts of sex. It is associated with manliness and it is the stimulus for development of testes, penises, hair, height and muscles.

The surprise is that women have testosterone too, secreted by the ovaries, just as it is secreted by the male testes. It helps women's sex-life as well as men's; in some cases where the ovaries have been removed (during a hysterectomy, for instance) sexual desire plummets and the whole quality of life suffers. Testosterone patches have been found to improve well-being all round. Donatella Marazziti, a psychiatrist at the University of Pisa in Italy, has found that testosterone levels rise in women and fall in men when they are in love. So there is a harmonizing of hormones.

LIVE FAST, DIE YOUNG – LIVE SLOW, DIE ANYWAY.

Phenylethylamine

The thrill of bungee-jumping, sky-diving, roller-coaster riding or skiing gives a great buzz. For many it is addictive, they can't get enough of it. Rather like serial lovers, as it turns out. To accompany the thrill of the dangerous sport, the brain secretes a hormone, phenylethylamine (PEA), which has an effect similar to amphetamine. During the first heady days of passionate love your brain is awash with PEA. It works at the nerve synapses, speeding up the transmission of nerve impulses, so the overall effect is that everything is enhanced. Colours are brighter, sounds are richer, the world is a wonderful place thanks to the 'love drug' PEA.

So the high of sky-diving is a similar exhilaration to the high of falling in love (possibly why we 'fall' in love and don't 'climb' into it).

Dangerous sports are therefore a substitute for love. As Piet Hein, the Danish scientist and poet, put it:

The human spirit sublimates
The impulses it thwarts.
A healthy sex life mitigates
The lust for other sports.

The discovery of the chemical link between danger and love makes one think. Could this be why we take our girl-friends on fairground rides; so that they get their PEA high, then look at us and feel love? Could Romeo have fallen so easily for Juliet if he wasn't indulging in dangerous love at the Capulets' ball? Might the popular practice of lovers throwing themselves off a cliff be a last-ditch attempt to recreate that loving buzz?

FORGET LOVE. I'D RATHER FALL IN CHOCOLATE!

Chocoholism

Here's why we love chocolate: chocolate contains PEA! The PEA in chocolate is the reason why we give them to our beloveds, why we eat them ourselves in vast quantities when our beloveds have dumped us, and why chocolate manufacturers are never completely unhappy during economic recessions – sales always go up when nations are depressed.

NOTHING TAKES THE TASTE OUT OF PEANUT BUTTER QUITE LIKE UNREQUITED LOVE.

(Charlie Brown)

Why food loses its taste

What an impact a slap in the face can have. All the bright colours have gone, except the bright scarlet on your cheek. The heavenly choir is replaced by a ringing in the ear. Testosterone, oestrogen, PEA, dopamine, adrenaline – all turned firmly off now. While they were up they gave that feeling of euphoria, that heightening of the sensations that goes with passion.

Colours were brighter, music was more musical, tastes were tastier. Now they are absent from your life so, although the peanut butter is the same chemically as it ever was, it is nothing more than a brown paste that coats the tongue. Now, instead of living to eat, you eat merely to live. Until the next time.

SLOW FOOD

TRUE LOVE IS WHEN YOU PUT SOMEONE ON A PEDESTAL, AND THEY FALL – BUT YOU ARE THERE TO CATCH THEM.

Serotonin

One sign of infatuation is that you cannot find any fault with your partner. Love is truly blind. I expect you can think of many couples around you who are quite unsuited to each other. 'Quite frankly I don't understand what she sees in him' is a common enough comment heard in your vicinity in the past year, I'll bet. But *your* partner is not like the others. He's perfect. I should point out that the vision you have is slightly drug-enhanced; the drug is serotonin.

Serotonin is a hormone whose function was discovered in the 1940s, when it was noticed that depressives and people suffering from Obsessive Compulsive Disorder (OCD) had low serotonin levels. Obsessives often repeat actions over and over – checking that doors are locked or endlessly washing, unable to focus on ordinary life. As a side effect they are often depressed, sometimes suicidally, and make bad judgements. Giving doses of serotonin reduces the obsessive behaviour.

The doctors involved in this research couldn't help noticing that the symptoms of the OCD sufferers were very similar to those of people hopelessly in love. Could it be that serotonin plays a part in passion? Yes, indeed; it seems that it is lowered levels of serotonin in lovers that produce fantasizing, obsessive thoughts, mood swings from depression to elation, just like OCD. Taking a drug which raises the level of serotonin makes you saner. It aids rational judgement, critical thinking, intelligent decisions and cuts down the fantasizing. Unsurprisingly, it also makes erections impossible. Yes, serotonin is the madam of your mind, the maiden auntie on your cerebral sofa. Love dies when it turns up. This is why it's impossible to be in love and sane at the same time. Either you have to be mad or you can be rational.

YOU DON'T LOVE A WOMAN BECAUSE SHE IS BEAUTIFUL, SHE IS BEAUTIFUL BECAUSE YOU LOVE HER.

(Oscar Hammerstein)

Serotonin at work

Dear Editor

My best friend has been brainwashed. He is in love with a woman who is, frankly, plain. And she has the wrong-shaped nose. How can he be so blind? It is embarrassing for everyone to be in the same room as a nose that big. She is clearly plying him with mind–altering drugs. All they do all day is giggle and write poems to each other and (YUK!) touch. What can be done to rescue my friend?

Dear Reader

The mind–altering drug to which you refer is serotonin. Because your friend's serotonin levels are lowered, he is not being overly critical of his love because of her nose. And a good thing too. Can you imagine how wonderful it must be for her? Having lived for so long among men like you, who treat her badly simply because of the size of her nose, she has found someone who has spotted her intelligence, sensitivity and wit. If they have babies, they will be brought up in a laughing, caring home. This is exactly what those love drugs evolved for, to bond people so completely that the resulting babies have the greatest possible chance of achieving full potential. He's not hallucinating when he sees her beauty; you are when you don't.

HE FELT NOW THAT HE WAS NOT SIMPLY CLOSE TO HER, BUT THAT HE DID NOT KNOW WHERE HE ENDED AND SHE BEGAN.

(Leo Tolstoy)

Mirror Neurons

There is an exercise, which actors carry out in rehearsals, called 'The Mirror'. One actor becomes the mirror of the other, doing exactly what they do. When it goes well, you can't tell which one is the mirror – both seem to be able to predict perfectly how the other is going to move. Love is like this all the time. The two become one, thoughts and feelings roll along side by side in perfect harmony. The mirror neurons are reflecting each other completely.

Personal space is normally heavily guarded. An invisible no-go zone surrounds you. You can allow any amount of manoeuvrings outside the boundary, but once they've crossed the border a personal space invader is repelled either by aggression and signs of anxiety, or by delicately stepping backwards away from the trespasser. For the chosen one, though, there is all-zones clearance. By these two means you are removing the boundaries between you. You are, as the cliché has it, an item.

WE ARE ALL A LITTLE WEIRD AND LIFE'S A LITTLE WEIRD, AND WHEN WE FIND SOMEONE WHOSE WEIRDNESS IS COMPATIBLE WITH OURS, WE JOIN UP WITH THEM AND FALL IN MUTUAL WEIRDNESS AND CALL IT LOVE.

Oxytocin and Vasopressin

Between two committed lovers there is no disagreement, no surprise, but deep understanding and pleasure, brought about by oxytocin and vasopressin, two similar hormones whose precise functions are not known, but which accompany loving thoughts about family, babies and lovers, according to fMRI (brain) scans.

Oxytocin is released during orgasm, during labour and when breast feeding. So it would appear to be a very family-oriented hormone.

Vasopressin, in particular, has been linked to marital devotion through studies of two closely related voles: the prairie vole, which is devoted to its mate, and its cousin the field vole, which isn't. Researchers at the Yerkes National Primate Research Center of Emory University and Atlanta's Center for Behavioral Neuroscience managed to increase the number of vasopressin receptors in one of the field vole's principal reward regions, the ventral pallidum, and the result was dramatic – the cad became miraculously monogamous. What little we know of vasopressin stems from this study, so it is too early to form any conclusions for humans. But you can imagine the sales potential for a vasopressin spray, which wives can use on their men just before they leave home in the morning.

LOVE MAKES TIME PASS; TIME MAKES LOVE PASS.

Perception of time

Doesn't time fly when you're having fun, goes the saying. What it really means is this: we have no real conception of time. We never needed to evolve one, because in the past we paced ourselves by the sun (we have an internal clock to do that which measures a 'circadian rhythm' of approximately 24 hours). But accurate pacing out of hours is a recent notion. Without any metering of the time, we have to guess. When we are having fun with a loved one, who fills our mind with music and rainbows, there isn't enough day for us. Juliet can't believe her night with Romeo has been so short:

Wilt thou be gone? it is not yet near day:
    It was the nightingale, and not the lark,
That pierced the fearful hollow of thine ear;
    Nightly she sings on yon pomegranate tree:
Believe me, love, it was the nightingale.

As Einstein, the master of flexi-time, put it: 'When a man sits with a pretty girl for an hour, it seems like a minute. But let him sit on a hot stove for a minute and it's longer than any hour. That's relativity.'

ABSENCE MAKES THE HEART GO WANDER.

How to dampen love

In Juliet's time the solution for parents whose children got involved in unwanted liaisons was to send them on a long journey across Europe in the hope that their passion would be spent by the time they returned. In most cases this did the trick. The magic of the first romantic weeks, with the flood of chemical and tactile signals which accompanied it, evoked a wonderful vivid memory. But without direct contact with the beloved the hormones die down, and so the emotional colours of love fade, leaving just that

MARCO POLO WRITES TO HIS BELOVED
NOW MARRIED WITH 3 KIDS...

wonderful memory, then a pretty nice memory, then a distant memory; never quite as strong as the real thing.

Far apart, the young folk now appraise each other more coolly. It is well known that when someone sits down to write a list of their lover's pros and cons, the relationship is already doomed. Love just doesn't work when the hormones are back in the cupboard.

THE NITTY GRITTY

Why sexual reproduction?

Wouldn't podding be better? Then we wouldn't have to bother with sex. You would stop what you were doing for a moment, divide down the middle, show your other half to the door, wave him (or, rather, it) goodbye and settle down to the paper again. It's so fast as well. Instead of two of you having to work together to make a baby using sexual reproduction, you could do it in separate rooms and double the baby rate. Actually, asexual reproduction is even better than that, since the new generation would divide again to make four, then eight, then sixteen . . . You could take over the world, eat the food and drive the sexual reproducers to extinction.

The problem is that asexual reproduction produces an unvaryingly uniform kind of population. You live on a planet where bacteria, fungi, viruses and parasites are all determined to get you, and will mutate frantically to break through your defences (see p.91). If you don't keep

AT THE RATE AMOEBAS DIVIDE, FAST FOOD CAN'T BE FAST ENOUGH

ducking and weaving, genetically speaking, you will succumb sooner or later. And it won't be just you that succumbs, it'll be your entire extended family, so you can kiss your species goodbye. Perhaps, then, we should consider sexual reproduction.

SEX IS HEREDITARY. IF YOUR PARENTS NEVER HAD IT, CHANCES ARE YOU WON'T EITHER.

Sexual vs. asexual reproduction

There is a way to see the advantage of sexual reproduction laid out panoramically before us because some animals can choose how to reproduce, sexually or asexually. Scientists have studied the circumstances under which they change. One such species is the worm *nais pardalis*, found in the lakes near the nuclear power station at Chernobyl, in the Ukraine. On 13 April 2003, *New Scientist* reported that since the explosion of the nuclear reactor in 1986 the worms had started to change their sexual behaviour: until then they had been reproducing asexually, but since the explosion they had switched strongly into sexual mode. The change was greater the closer they were to the power station. The most likely explanation is that the polluted water near the nuclear pile was so toxic that the worm population was frantically varying its genetic make-up to try and find a strain that could survive in the new conditions. Once a successful son had been bred, he, she or it would change back to asexual reproduction to bulk out numbers.

We humans don't have the option to switch like those worms, and considering the importance of variation through the generations, we have chosen the correct option. Sexual reproduction it is, so sex there will have to be.

TELLING A TEENAGER THE FACTS OF LIFE IS LIKE GIVING A FISH A BATH.

(Arnold H. Glasow)

Sex myths

It seems to be a parental rite of passage. At some stage all dads have to sit down with their sons, fumble and mumble for ten minutes before the comforting words are spoken: 'It's all right, Dad, I know.'

But are kids actually as wise about sex as they say? There are many myths abroad, some preposterous, some very dangerous:

- Jumping up and down after sex will stop a girl getting pregnant.
- You can't get pregnant the first time you have sex.
- A cure for HIV is to have sex with a virgin.
- You will kill off the sperm if you wear a luminous watch during sex (on your penis).
- Masturbation causes blindness, syphilis, bags under the eyes and/or hairy palms of the hand. And is a sign of homosexuality.
- Only gay men get AIDS.
- Sex is impossible over the age of forty.
- STDs can be caught off lavatory seats.
- Losing weight makes the penis bigger.
- Eating aphrodisiacs – oysters, horny goat weed, ginseng, rhino horn, ginkgo, kava kava, palmetto berries, bananas, truffles and asparagus – will make sex more enjoyable, although it will probably cause the bed to break.

Absolutely none of the above is true, apart from the one about the bed breaking, but all of them have advocates. Many a rhino could testify against the rhino-horn aphrodisiac claim, if it were not dead. Tragically, the notion that sex with a virgin cures HIV is widespread in southern Africa, where it is contributing to the crisis. The ignorance is dangerous, proper sex education is essential, but many governments and churches worldwide believe that talking about sex will turn the nation wildly promiscuous, so all is silence (see p. 123).

The best time to give the talk about sex is when the child asks, usually when they are two. You might as well give them the facts straight away, then it won't come as a shock later. There are many books available which are not only pleasant and instructive for the wee toddler but also not too embarrassing for Dad.

LIFE WITHOUT SEX MIGHT BE SAFER BUT IT WOULD BE UNBEARABLY DULL. IT IS THE SEX INSTINCT WHICH MAKES WOMEN SEEM BEAUTIFUL, WHICH THEY ARE ONCE IN A BLUE MOON, AND MEN SEEM WISE AND BRAVE, WHICH THEY NEVER ARE AT ALL. THROTTLE IT, DENATURALIZE IT, TAKE IT AWAY, AND HUMAN EXISTENCE WOULD BE REDUCED TO THE PROSAIC, LABORIOUS, BORESOME, IMBECILE LEVEL OF LIFE IN AN ANTHILL.

(H. L. Mencken)

Sex is central

It seems that sexual reproduction is of practical use. That would explain why it's so much fun. It would explain quite a lot besides. The courtship rituals we have been looking at amount to a smidge of the whole picture. Look at the average high street: those shops full of jewellery, clothing, music, cookery, drink, cars, fine art, all the organizations peddling ballet, theatre, opera, parties and festivals all flourish because of the need to attract mates and mate with them.

After years of studious deployment of all these lures, you are lying next to your loved one doing what comes naturally – and believe me, even with no knowledge of sex at all, humans can eventually work out what to do. Quite soon you will be returning to the real world, which will be – pace Henry Mencken – prosaic, laborious, boresome and imbecilic, but it will be more tolerable for the knowledge deep inside you that you have done what your genes set out to do when you were fourteen.

LOVE IS AN EXPLODING CIGAR WE WILLINGLY SMOKE.

(Lynda Barry)

The male orgasm

Love is a cigar which explodes in three ways. First, while you are falling in love your glands explode like a firework display inside you, spilling a heady mixture of hormones into the bloodstream. The pituitary, hypothalamus and adrenal glands, testes and ovaries all produce changes in the levels of serotonin, oxytocin, testosterone, vasopressin, phenylethylamine and opioids such as acetylcholine and dopamine.

Love-making climaxes with the second explosion. In men, fluid from the vas deferens, the prostate, the ampulla, and the seminal vesicles are propelled into the internal urethra by contractions of the groin muscles. The filling of the internal urethra signals from here are transmitted through the pudendal nerves from the spinal cord. Increases in pressure in the urethra cause the semen to be propelled to the exterior, resulting in orgasm.

The third explosion happens when your wife finds out about your affair.

COITO, ERGO SUM.

The female orgasm

The male orgasm is vital for the injection of sperm into the vagina. But what about the female orgasm? It has long been held that the female orgasm is useful because muscular contractions help speed the sperm up the vaginal path towards the uterus, but some doubt has been cast on this recently. In her book *The Case of the Female Orgasm: Bias in the Science of Evolution*, Elisabeth Lloyd, professor of biology at Indiana University, points out that there is no link between a woman's ability to achieve orgasm during sex and her ability to produce babies. Indeed, many women struggle to climax during conventional penetrative sex, and usually do so only with direct clitoral stimulation. Yet during masturbation both women and men can achieve orgasm in about four minutes.

Lloyd suggests that the female orgasm may be merely a leftover from an earlier stage of human evolution. Like the male nipple, the female orgasm could be a relic, which had its uses in the past but now has only an ornamental function.

However, like the male nipple, one would feel the lack if it were not there.

SEX: THE PLEASURE IS MOMENTARY, THE POSITION RIDICULOUS, AND THE EXPENSE DAMNABLE.

(Lord Chesterfield)

Bestial beasts

Lord Chesterfield should be grateful to be human. Sex among other animals takes so many different forms, many of them dangerous, painful or lethal.

One's mind immediately turns to the spiny anteater, *Echidna*. How do they make love? Carefully! The female lies on her stomach and digs part of her front legs and head into the ground. The suitor digs a trench around her, while stroking the female with his front foot and attempting to lift her tail with a hind foot, all the while keeping an eye on those spines of hers. After four hours of this 'foreplay' the male will gingerly get himself on his side with his tail under hers, a position that allows him to extend his four-headed penis into her cloaca.

The bed bug, *Cimex lectularius*, must be the most brutal of lovers. Without any attempt at courtship the male pounces on the female, stabbing her in the side of the abdomen with his genitalia. 'Traumatic insemination' has evolved as a means for males to take control of reproduction away from females. By stabbing the female in the abdomen they circumvent female semen-storage organs, female secretions, not to mention female behaviour aimed at deciding whether or not to use a male's sperm.

The orb spider male inserts his two pedipalps, loaded with sperm, into the female's two vaginal openings, inflates them so they cannot be removed, then dies. The female often has to eat the male simply so that she can go about her business.

A breed of fly, *Serromyia femorata*, takes up a position during sex, which resembles kissing, but, at the end of mating, the female sucks out the body content of the male through his mouth.

The male redback spider somersaults into his lover's fangs and insists on being eaten. If she spits him out, he jumps right back in again.

The female fishing spider (*Dolomedes triton*) often eats her mate *before* sex. Curiously, it is not as endangered a species as it ought to be.

We all know about the poor male mantis. He has to be careful in his initial approach, but provided he has mounted the female *before* she begins to devour his head, he will successfully complete copulation by the time she has eaten the rest of him.

WHAT IS THE DIFFERENCE BETWEEN MEN AND WOMEN? A WOMAN WANTS ONE MAN TO SATISFY HER EVERY NEED, AND A MAN WANTS EVERY WOMAN TO SATISFY HIS ONE NEED.

Sex records in the animal kingdom

How does the male sex urge in humans compare with other animals?

Rodents reign supreme when it comes to repeated mating. A type of gerbil called Shaw's Jird (Meriones *shawi*) has been observed to copulate 224 times in the space of two hours.

Length of bond: *Deroceras gorgonium* (a slug found in Greece) seems to hold the record for the shortest bout of passion, at one second. Whereas the longest we know of is that of the lowly stick insect (of the *Phasmida* family), which goes on for several months. The male attaches himself to the female's back, which allows her to continue living her life while he's at it.

The blue whale claims the record for the longest penis, at just over 3 metres (9 ft) long and 30 cm (12 inches) in diameter, weighing 50 kg (110 lb). No surprise there. If you take measurements as a percentage of body length things are a little different. Goose barnacles, with inch-and-a-half-long appendages, rate about 150 per cent. Impressive, but the top banana is the Santa Cruz banana slug (*Ariolimax dolichophallus*) which is 25 cm (10 inches) long and possesses an 82.5 cm (2.7 ft) penis, or over 300 per cent its body length.

The prize for the biggest balls goes to the northern right whale (*Eubalaena glacialis*), which has a pair of gonads that can weigh up to 1,000 kg (2,205 lb). The enormous size is an evolutionary adaptation caused by 'sperm competition'. When the female whale comes into heat, she is immediately mobbed by thirty or so males who shove one another as they try to jockey into position. When one male finishes (typically this takes 30 seconds), another moves in. And another. The hope of each is to wash out a competitor's sperm with unknown gallons of their own, thereby ensuring that their genes will win through.

But the longest sperm belongs to one of the smallest animals. A breed of fruit fly, *Drosophila bifurca*, has sperm 6 cm (2.4 inches) long, which is 1,000 times longer than a human sperm and twenty times longer than the fly.

The largest vagina in the world belongs to the blue whale, predictably, since she has to accommodate the biggest penis in the world. Judged as a percentage of body mass, though, the undisputed winner is a parasitic nematode worm, the bumblebee threadworm (*Sphaerularia bombi*) that seeks out a queen bee as a host (hence its name). After settling in, her reproductive apparatus begins to expand within the bee, until it is around 2 cm (1 inch) long. Up to thirty times the length of the original worm and 300 times the volume – an overall increase of 30,000 per cent.

Number of offspring: a single giant puffball may contain 7 trillion spores, and a single large shaggy ink cap (mushroom) contains enough spores to stretch 41 miles if laid end to end.

The modest human male can boast that his apparatus is bigger in proportion to his overall size than most other animals, and certainly than all other apes, but aside from that he ought to keep pretty quiet.

A HARD MAN IS GOOD TO FIND.

(Mae West)

Finding a partner in the animal kingdom

Many animals are facing extinction. The problem is worst for those who live a solitary life for most of the year and have a short period in season. For the female panda, if a male does not find her while she is in oestrus, that's another year lost. Pandas are critically endangered; the loss of their habitat has left so few of them in the wild that finding each other is becoming nearly impossible. The panda's predicament is serious, but still better than that of Lonesome George.

So far as we know there is only one Lonesome George. George is a 1.5 metre (5 ft) long, 90 kg (200 lb) tortoise aged between 60 and 200. In 1971 he was discovered on the remote Galapagos island of Pinta, from which tortoises had supposedly been exterminated by buccaneering whalers and seal hunters. A desperate worldwide search is underway for a mate, but the urgency of his situation is lost on poor George, who has shown no interest in any of the females provided.

The Osedax has one answer. The Osedax is a deep-sea worm often found munching on whale bones. Since there aren't a lot of these, the chances of finding a meal and a mate together are vanishingly small. They have solved the problem by simply having one or two tiny husbands living inside them, so they can have sex and supper at the same time.

Animals are often unhappy with just one set of sex organs. The tapeworm has a complete set of male and female organs in each segment of its body. Each set copulates independently, and the resulting eggs are washed away by the host's digestive wastes. The longest recorded tapeworm was 70 metres (230 ft) long, with 11,000 segments, so that means this one worm had 22,000 individual sex organs.

LITERATURE IS MOSTLY ABOUT HAVING SEX AND NOT MUCH ABOUT HAVING CHILDREN; LIFE IS THE OTHER WAY AROUND.

(David Lodge)

Sex on the mind (M)

Men, famously, think about sex every six seconds. In that broad sweeping way that they often have, evolutionary psychologists endow this with an evolutionary advantage. For man, the further and wider he can distribute his gametes the more his genes will be passed on. Evolution must surely favour promiscuity. However, as we know from the reality, promiscuity is not nearly as rife as the evolutionary psychologists would predict. It appears that there is a down side. If the nation as a whole is preoccupied with sex, sex and nothing but sex, then fights between rivals, mooning over lovers and the general obsessions and compulsions of which the mind is capable take over everyone's life, and not a yam gets mashed. So among humans the urge for sex has to be offset by the urge to care for the results of sex. Taking time off from promiscuity to mind the babies is a better way to ensure the survival to the next generation.

NYMPHOMANIAC: A WOMAN AS OBSESSED WITH SEX AS AN AVERAGE MAN.

(Mignon McLaughlin)

Sex on the mind (F)

The notion that ladies don't like sex is as likely as the notion that they don't fart. The course of evolution has landed all of us with an enthusiasm for sex, whatever our gender. The more enthusiastic participants produce the more enthusiastic offspring, so levels of lust should rise with each new generation. Despite the fact that birth rates have been declining for over a century, that is certainly the popular perception. Each new generation firmly believes that lust is on the increase and their era is the most promiscuous ever. The Victorians boasted a famous prurience – swathing their girls in frocks and petticoats so that not an ankle could be seen, even covering up table legs in case they should induce lewd thoughts in the men-folk – and encouraged strict abstinence from sex until properly married. But the reality was anything but decorous, with parish records around England showing between 10 per cent and 25 per cent of baptisms being out of wedlock.

John Major, Britain's Prime Minister during the 1990s, campaigned for 'family values', but a series of sex scandals within his own government, including the discovery that he had only just finished having an affair with one of his own Cabinet ministers, rather took the wind out of his sails. Meanwhile, sex sails on regardless.

LIFE IN LUBBOCK, TEXAS, TAUGHT ME TWO THINGS: ONE IS THAT GOD LOVES YOU AND YOU'RE GOING TO BURN IN HELL. THE OTHER IS THAT SEX IS THE MOST AWFUL, FILTHY THING ON EARTH AND YOU SHOULD SAVE IT FOR SOMEONE YOU LOVE.

(Butch Hancock)

Religious and political leaders tend to dislike sex education because a) it removes the romance from romantic love, b) it might lead to the use of contraception, and c), most importantly, talking about sex will cause all children to indulge in it next break-time.

The central thing to remember is that sex will happen. The human organism, brain and body, has evolved with procreation as its single goal. All the rest is propaganda. So either sex happens in ignorance or it happens with knowledge. The puritans must grip the arms of their settees, grit their teeth and allow children of twelve to be introduced to methods of contraception.

Sweden radically changed its sex education policies in 1975. Recommendations of abstinence and sex-only-within-marriage were dropped, contraceptive education was made explicit, and a nationwide network of youth clinics was established specifically to provide confidential contraceptive advice and free contraceptives to young people. Over the next two decades, Sweden saw its teenage birth rate fall by 80 per cent. Sexually transmitted diseases also fell by 40 per cent in the 1990s. With sex, as with the laws of the land, ignorance should be no excuse.

A BIG DIFFERENCE BETWEEN SEX FOR MONEY AND SEX FOR FREE IS THAT SEX FOR MONEY USUALLY COSTS LESS.

(Brendan Francis)

Prostitution

Prostitution happens too, very often because women need money to support their children, and because men are willing to pay the money. And it isn't confined to humans: even penguins have been seen to indulge in what should technically be termed prostitution, exchanging sex for nesting materials.

But it begs a question. We have seen that when it comes to picking a sexual partner, women find wealth or power a strong attractant (see Kissinger's views on power as aphrodisiac, p. 68). And we see a practical reason for that, in the successful raising of children. So what is the difference? On the one hand a prostitute will offer sex for money; on the other hand a mother receives money from her sexual partner.

One important difference lies with the emotions. Prostitution involves sex with no emotions – no exploding cigar. As Mae West put it, 'It's a business doing pleasure with you.' The rearing of a child within a family involves emotions of all sorts: the joy of sharing as well as the agony of disagreeing; the protectiveness of the bond as well as the loneliness of separation; the joy of sex as well as the fierce jealousy of suspicion. Those emotions may be a maelstrom, but they are there for a good reason – raising baby bunting.

NEVER SLEEP WITH ANYONE CRAZIER THAN YOURSELF.

Bonding and sex

If all goes well, as far as the selfish gene is concerned, then you will not only have had a beautiful night, exquisite petting, kissing and orgasms, you will also have changed in other ways, which will still be enveloping you at breakfast. Oxytocin is produced in large quantities during orgasm, and it is produced again in smaller dollops in each other's company, when you touch, hug and talk. Oxytocin has been labelled the 'trust drug'. When administered to experimental subjects prior to a risk game, they showed greater levels of trust than other subjects. It is thought to suppress the actions of the amygdala, the area of the brain responsible for fear and panic.

On the morning after the night before your minds are still suffused with oxytocin. Gradually your equilibrium will be re-established, during which time you will discover that your partner is demented. This may take weeks, it may take minutes, but alongside this purely intellectual knowledge sits the stronger, hormonal knowledge that sex with them is fun. The oxytocin will see to it that the sex continues. You will hate each other. You will adore each other. You will cast your eyes to heaven and mutter 'can't live with him, can't live without him'. You will, of course, be quite normal.

LOVE IS A MATTER OF CHEMISTRY, SEX IS A MATTER OF PHYSICS.

Can sex be explained scientifically?

One reason why real people hate scientists is that they take the romance away from everything. Art is a matter of pigments and photons, music is complex air vibrations, love is merely molecules, plus added levers and forces. And a little hydraulics.

Many psychologists have tried to reduce human behaviour to mathematical formulae. The American experimental psychologist Clark Hull dominated the field for many years in the 1940s and 1950s. He tried fanatically hard to formulate a precise mathematical model which would identify just how much of behaviour is due to what. His descriptions of behaviour were full of drive-habit strengths, unconditioned responses, fractional anticipatory goal responses, laid out in mathematically precise formulae – all desperate attempts to nail down the cloud of whims and fancies which is human behaviour. His research didn't even work for rats in a T-maze, let alone humans.

But although the task of understanding the brain is inconceivably difficult for our brains to comprehend, we should still remind ourselves that our emotions are not a quasi-religious, out-of-body experience controlled by a spiritual force beyond our power to control or understand, but stem from hormones, and that evolution created these hormones.

This may take some of the magic out of the joy, but it will also take some pain out of the misery at the end of the romance. That same army of emotions which lifted you above the stars when you were in love will cast you into the darkest abyss when the affair is over. To know that it's all just a load of chemicals will now be of some small comfort.

THE ONLY PART THE HEART PLAYS IN LOVE IS TO MARK THE MID-POINT BETWEEN THE BRAIN AND THE GROIN.

Where love lies — the truth

Perhaps it's time to redesign the Valentine's Day card. The use of a heart symbol to indicate emotions is seriously out of date. In Aristotle's day, 2,500 years ago, the heart was the centre of everything, both spatially and in terms of hierarchy. It was the part that is formed first in embryological development. It was the source of bodily heat and primarily responsible for nutritive functions. And it was the seat of emotions and sensations, for it housed the 'central sense organ', a kind of coordinating centre that processes the information received from the peripheral sense organs (through the blood vessels), and issued decisions to the limbs and other parts of the body involved in action and motion. The brain, on the other hand, had the task of merely cooling the blood, like a car radiator. Less than a century later, Galen, in Alexandria, had proved that the brain was the source of thinking and emotions, but the damage was done, and from then on the belief that the heart was so much more than a mere pump was everywhere. Hence the use of a heart on Valentine's Day cards.

Now that we know the seat of emotions is a section of the brain called the limbic system, we should bite the bullet and portray it on our Valentine's Day cards. I think the recipient of one of these will be in no doubt about the feelings of the sender.

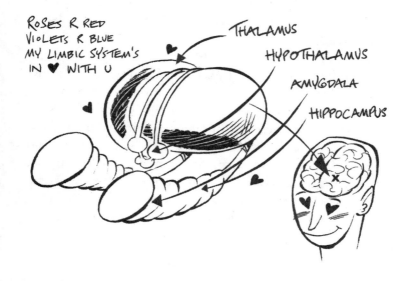

ROSES R RED
VIOLETS R BLUE
MY LIMBIC SYSTEM'S
IN ♥ WITH U

THALAMUS

HYPOTHALAMUS

AMYGDALA

HIPPOCAMPUS

LIFE IS A SEXUALLY TRANSMITTED DISEASE.

Sexually transmitted diseases (other than life)

When you think about it, STDs have chosen an absolutely brilliant way to get about. You see, life as a normal pathogen is never completely safe. If you are a contagious disease, you have to hang around on someone's hand until they touch someone else – you hop on the hand – and then you hold your breath, waiting for them to put their finger in their mouth. And there's always the chance that your host will wash his hands and ruin everything.

On the other hand, as it were, if you are an *infectious* disease you are sneezed into the air – and then what? You are at the whim of the breeze. You could end up trying to infect a floorboard.

As an STD you have it much easier. Your home is warm, wet and dark, just as you like it, and you get to be transferred directly – pumped, rubbed and injected into your new home. All you have to worry about is whether your host will make love, and you can be certain that he or she is working tirelessly towards that end most of the day and night. This is good news for gonorrhoea, chlamydia, syphilis, genital warts, genital herpes, AIDS, hepatitis, vaginitis, and numerous lesser known and less lethal critters, but not such good news for your host's new lover.

WEDDING PRESCIENCE

Our bower-bird friend, who showed us the way to strut our stuff and impress the ladies, has no very useful advice when it comes to marriage. For him and for many animals the marriage is over straight after the consummation. The evolutionary advantage of sticking around is lost on him. Mammals, however, and particularly humans, need to take time looking after their children.

It all comes down to brain size. Animals with smaller brains must rely on instincts – built-in, automatic responses. Mammals, with their larger brains, can modify their behaviour. So while the fly will continuously bash its head against a glass pane, the dog will deduce that it can't get through that way, and an ape will work out how to open the window. But the ape's intuition doesn't come automatically. Apes (including the hairless sort) need time to learn the ways of the world; that's why they have longer childhoods.

The wedding ceremony ties the couple in with a community of people who have experiences they are dying to share with the next generation. Now the happy couple will be surrounded by a small army of friends, relatives and professionals, each of whom will give advice or help. All of them are useful for a young family in a half-decent world, and when times are hard they are absolutely vital.

But what about that strangely modern concept, the childless couple, who want to carry on working for a few years to build up a proper career and mortgage before having babies? The family without offspring was not something evolution would have planned for. You have evolved to produce a baby in nine months on the dot. Will the old instincts work in the new format?

IF IT WERE NOT FOR THE PRESENTS, ELOPEMENT WOULD BE PREFERABLE.

(G. Ade)

The wedding

Weddings are nerve-racking in a thousand ways, not least because the two gene pools, his and hers, will mix for perhaps the first time as a stream of cousins and uncles from both families mingle at the ceremony. (I wonder what is made of all the major histocompatibility complexes wafting around.) In a new marriage there are often reflections to be found of the bride and groom's parents' own marriages. On p.6 we saw that children can be so used to their family environment that they feel nervous away from it. On p.72 we saw that people tend to pick partners who remind them of their parents in certain key ways. We might therefore expect the two clans to be similar. Wedding ceremonies are the chance to mix the ingredients, to see how the chemistry works.

IT DOESN'T REALLY MATTER WHOM ONE MARRIES; ONE IS SURE TO FIND OUT NEXT MORNING THAT IT WAS SOMEBODY ELSE.

(Will Rogers)

A day later

What a pity so many couples these days are indulging in sex before the wedding night. The true drama of that first naked encounter is lost to them. As her eyelashes, hair extensions, falsies and make-up are being removed, what runs through his mind? And does she still love him, even without his toupee or teeth? Yes, the acting is over, the props are discarded. On that magic heavenly journey he finds that ladies can fart, she discovers that men snore. Armpits the world over need to be washed occasionally. And yet they still love each other. The love drugs such as oxytocin that their brains produce during love-making make them feel elated, relaxed and confident in each other's company. If it were not for hormones they would treat each other like quite good friends, but argue about who was going to sleep on the bed and who on the sofa.

Ruskin's wedding disaster

John Ruskin, the famous nineteenth-century art critic and champion of the Pre-Raphaelite artists, had an oxytocin-free wedding night in 1848, which has been the staple of gossip in artistic circles ever since. He was shocked and disgusted to find that his bride, Effie, had pubic hair.

Now Ruskin must have reckoned he knew what a naked lady looked like. He had come across enough of them in all those paintings. But he hadn't allowed for the universal convention that pubic hair is not to appear in pictures. Apart from a couple of slips, most notably Goya's *La Maja Desnuda*, that convention held world-wide. Ruskin was so shocked he had the marriage annulled immediately.

ALL MARRIAGES ARE HAPPY. IT'S THE LIVING TOGETHER AFTERWARD THAT CAUSES ALL THE TROUBLE.

(Raymond Hull)

A week later

There has been a slight shift. If the wedding was like winning the World Cup, metaphorically speaking, then the wedding night was like drinking champagne from it. But for the rest of the week you've been deciding who's going to do the washing up.

The change is tiny, probably getting lost in the thrash and pash of the honeymoon, but from the start there is a tiny, tremulous tint of jostling for the position of controller. Even in the best-ordered household, in fact especially in the best-ordered household, one will end up as the *capo di tutti*. Of course neither will admit to being *secondo*. To do so would be a humiliation and drive one straight to the bottle. Both, therefore, think they are on top. But in Chapter 2, pp. 21–38, on the difference between men and women, we see some of the flavour of the average home (with the by now saddle-sore proviso that most households are not average). He is bigger. She is more wily. He is therefore the commander, while she decides what he is going to command, and how.

So in marriages like this he will no doubt point out that she deals with the trivial things of life, like which house to buy, how to furnish it, where the children should go to school, etc., while he decides the really important issues, such as whether Sri Lanka should grant independence to the Tamils.

IN EVERY MARRIAGE MORE THAN A WEEK OLD, THERE ARE GROUNDS FOR DIVORCE. THE TRICK IS TO FIND, AND CONTINUE TO FIND, GROUNDS FOR MARRIAGE.

(Robert Anderson)

A month later

As the weeks pass by, the lovers resume their contact with the rest of the world and begin to function outside the love-nest. This brings the outside world into the home a little – as workloads increase, office schedules twine themselves around the mind and files fill the open spaces of the living room. Romantic suppers are reduced to candle-lit takeaways. You are never at home at the same time, it seems. This is what comes of career-building. But while you are building the career are you eroding your relationship? Without the oxytocin boosters of sex, petting and 'quality time' can you survive?

There is a danger that the hormones that provided the orchestra during courtship are not running at quite the same height now. You are beginning to change back again to the kind of person you were before you fell in love. Wow! That was a long time ago. So long ago that some of the slobby, selfish things you are doing now almost seem strange to you yourself. But real they are. And those selfish, irritating moments your partner has, they are the real McCoy too.

SUCCESSFUL MARRIAGE REQUIRES FALLING IN LOVE MANY TIMES, ALWAYS WITH THE SAME PERSON.

(Mignon McLaughlin)

Six months later

Don't give up. Love is never dead, only sleeping. The bonding continues whenever you do little things for each other. Little gifts, little hugs. Smiles. Jobs done. Oh, and when you've finished cleaning the Harley Davidson in the living room, wipe the oil off the curtains. All these little things will lure a few molecules of oxytocin out of their glands and make your lives a joy once more for a while.

And gifts. Giving presents is a tried and tested formula for connubial bliss. Masked boobies do it; the male, with great ceremony and much bowing, offers his beloved a pebble. Herons give their mates large twigs, the avian equivalent of buying her an ironing board. The male praying mantis, in a fine gesture of modesty, offers himself for supper. Needless to say theirs is a short marriage.

A note on gifts: you should always give her the kind of thing she likes. If she likes flowers you must bring home a bunch of flowers. If she really likes flowers and builds a garden with millions of flowers in it, you must still bring home a bunch of flowers. Things can get out of hand. If she once expressed an amused interest in frogs she will suddenly find years later that she now has a room entirely filled with froggy collectibles.

HOW CAN A WOMAN BE EXPECTED TO BE HAPPY WITH A MAN WHO INSISTS ON TREATING HER AS IF SHE WERE A PERFECTLY NORMAL HUMAN BEING

(Oscar Wilde)

A year later

Without that constant updating of affection, the cascade of emotions, which go with romance, cannot continue for ever. Up to an evolutionary eye-blink ago you would have had a baby by now, with a whole new set of bonding hormones and motivations. But without that extra kick, hormone fatigue must eventually set in. Oxytocin levels lessen and the emotional firework display ends, while the amygdala is allowed a freer rein, to add irritation, panic and disgust into the arena. Dopamine levels fall and the warmth of reward fades. Serotonin levels rise, the critic on the hearth begins to chirrup.

American humorist Helen Rowland said, 'Before marriage, a man will lay down his life for you; after marriage he won't even lay down his newspaper.' Both of you are becoming convinced that marriage is 'not a word, but a sentence'. You might get the unnerving feeling that, as Mary Tyler Moore said, 'Sometimes you have to get to know someone really well to realize you're really strangers.'

THE COURSE OF TRUE ANYTHING NEVER DOES RUN SMOOTH.

(Samuel Butler)

Two years later

Your family, friends and colleagues understand. They now think of you as a couple, talk to you as a couple, so it's impossible to be anything else. They will always be a reminder that you are together, even on days when you wish you had the whole planet between you. The group is a powerful force. In communities such as farming or fishing villages, where workmates are friends and friends are family, where everyone knows everyone else, there can be a lot of support and counselling from all generations. The older ones have been through the same troubles themselves so they can give advice, and the younger ones are learning the ways of the world by watching how you get on; for them you want to put on a good show.

If you don't have that inclusive community around then for you there are TV soaps. Soap opera storylines mirror life, so you will find yourself in there somewhere if you look hard enough. TV soaps can be seen as a natural product of evolution. The instinct for teamwork that mark humans out from other animals is still part of our genome, and is sublimated into soap opera storylines.

ONE ADVANTAGE OF MARRIAGE IS THAT, WHEN YOU FALL OUT OF LOVE WITH HIM OR HE FALLS OUT OF LOVE WITH YOU, IT KEEPS YOU TOGETHER UNTIL YOU FALL IN AGAIN.

(Judith Viorst)

Seven years later

Do you feel like divorcing? The law is here to help, by being slow, unfair and expensive. But if the legal profession is inadequate, think what a rabble they have to deal with. There are as many different divorce cases as there are people on the planet. As Tolstoy said, 'happy families are all alike; every unhappy family is unhappy in its own way'. Sorting out who is right and who is wrong when they fall out is very complicated, very lucrative for solicitors and therefore bankrupting for you.

When you come to think about it, if there are no children to consider, there is no logical reason why two married people should ever attempt the difficult feat of living together, except for fear of the other difficult feat, of divorce.

Socrates had the wisest words:

If you find a good partner you'll be happy; if not, you'll become a philosopher.

PLAYING AWAY

Prairie voles have been in the spotlight a lot recently, bless them. Ethologists have found out that they are monogamous. This condition, it turns out, is so rare in animals generally that it's practically kinky. Even their close relatives, the field voles, are as promiscuous as the rest of nature, so scientists are for ever hauling prairie voles and field voles out of their holes and doing tests on them to try and find the difference. What makes a love rat into a house mouse? We think we know the answer now (p. 103). We can only hope that the prairie voles' marriage will stand up to all the attention and publicity.

Are humans monogamous? No. Open any newspaper or listen to any pocket of gossip to hear the awful goings-on. Should we worry about it? Most zoologists would shrug their shoulders. Mammals are very rarely monogamous, even for a single breeding season. Dogs are, gibbons are, some South American monkeys, prairie voles of course . . . and already the list is pretty much complete. This understanding that animals are promiscuous is a modern one. Up

until recently we could point a camera at almost any pair of animals and be sure that we were coming away with a film of faithful couples toiling together to feed and protect their young: the robin redbreast and his mate, the squirrel and her squire. What those cameras missed was the secret dalliances, the furtive flings that just about every animal indulges in when the cameras (and mate) aren't watching. Females as well as males are up for it. Even in the classic chimp scenario, with the alpha male proudly protecting his harem, fighting to the death to keep lower males from them, the females will on occasions slip behind a tree with one of the juniors. All this we know through the magic of CCTV and cameras that have snuck into every possible hidey hole.

Ah, but not we humans, surely we stay faithful – except in very exceptional and well-publicized cases which bring shame on the generally good name of *Homo sapiens* – say the die-hards. Or so they used to say until the evidence became too compelling.

MONOGAMY LEAVES A LOT TO BE DESIRED.

Infidelity

The first crack in the façade came as far back as the 1940s, in a quiet maternity ward in a respectable US hospital, which must remain nameless to this day. During routine blood tests it was found that 10 per cent of the babies' blood types had elements not found in either the mother or her husband. The doctors knew what that meant, but the crack was hastily plastered over. The findings were not published. Surely they were an aberration. Later, sexual surveys from Alfred Kinsey (1948), Masters and Johnson (1966) and Shere Hite (1976) confirmed that, yes, we are every bit as promiscuous as that zoologist's shrug would suggest. Ten per cent; that's the score. Ten per cent of us have dads who are not our fathers.

YOU KNOW THAT THE TASMANIANS, WHO NEVER COMMITTED ADULTERY, ARE NOW EXTINCT.

(W. Somerset Maugham)

The scientific explanation for infidelity

Evolutionary biologists can provide a scientific explanation for male infidelity. (It is this tendency to explain infidelity, rather than out-and-out condemn it, that gives evolution-ary biologists a bad name.) The 'aim' of evolution is to get as many babies born as possible. The more offspring a male can beget, the more his genes will spread. Bringing up your own babies is time-consuming and expensive, particularly if they are going to be hanging around the house for the next twenty years. What better plan than to get somebody else to do the bringing up. From the male point of view, infidelity gives an evolutionary advantage, which is why men keep on being unfaithful to their partners, not because they are evil but because they are slaves to their genetic destiny. (Please do not try to use this argument in court.)

INFIDELITY IS THE APPLICATION OF DEMOCRACY TO LOVE.

(H. L. Mencken)

Are women as promiscuous as men?

A man could in his lifetime have 15,000 orgasms, and sire 15,000 children. In fact the record for fathering children is the eighteenth-century Emperor Moulay Ismail the Bloodthirsty of Morocco with 888 little darlings. Normally we don't try that hard. The average number of children per family in Britain is 1.99.

For women the situation is quite different, of course. Mums could be stuck with the unexpected consequences of infidelity for at least the next nine months, so you would expect them to be much more chary about adulterous relationships. However, it takes two to tango, and all available surveys put the female infidelity rate somewhere around half that of males. This figure appears to be worldwide, and not to be a recent phenomenon, so we may assume that female infidelity did, does and will happen in spite of the dangers of pregnancy.

TO OUR MISTRESSES AND WIVES. MAY THEY NEVER MEET.

Why are women adulterous?

So, can the evolutionary psychologists offer any solution, any cast-iron, mathematically sound account for female infidelity? There are three possible explanations, all of which strike us in our comfortable world as eccentric, but for more arduous times make excellent survival sense. Out in the early savannah, our hominid ancestors lived a harsh life, with starvation and disease a constant threat. Then, to have more than one mate made sense because:

1) The man could well die suddenly from predation, fighting, accident or disease. For the woman to put all her eggs in one basket would be to risk losing the sole provider;
2) In the struggle to combat parasites, the more genetic diversity the better, and polygamy is a gene mixer;

3) Having a number of male providers means extra gifts of food and support for the children.

With all these excuses tucked in their belts, one has to say that humanity's infidelity rate is not as high as it might be. Ten per cent is a figure to be a little bit smug about perhaps, unless your partner is one of the ten percenters.

MOTHERHOOD IS A MATTER OF FACT, FATHERHOOD IS A MATTER OF OPINION.

The mystery of concealed ovulation

There are three big differences between humans and pretty much every other animal. First, we don't appear to have an off-season for sex. In all other animals, ovulation, and therefore sex, occurs for very short periods only. Humans, however, can have an active sex life all year round for seventy years. Second, although the female of the species is only fertile for a short time every month, she gives no clue as to when that is. This concealed ovulation is another puzzle for the evolutionary scientist. Third, while all other animals are quite blatant about their copulation, it is a private activity for humans. (Even Paul McCartney's song 'Why Don't We Do It in the Road', lewd and blatant as it is, has the comforting line, 'No one will be watching us'.)

Together, these factors mean that nobody but the woman herself can know when she is having sex, with whom, and whether she was ovulating at the time. Why so? Jared Diamond, in *The Rise and Fall of the Third Chimpanzee*, lists no less than six possible explanations for concealed ovulation in early man.

1) Concealed ovulation evolved to reduce aggression among the males. Because they couldn't be sure of their parenthood or that of their offspring, sexual competition and rivalry was pointless, so they fought each other less and cooperated more in the important things, such as hunting.

2) Concealed ovulation and constant receptivity in females evolved to cement her bonds with her male, through the continuous reward of love-making.

3) Chimps in oestrus receive gifts of food and protection from their males. A female human's continuous oestrus – or at least its appearance – ensures continuous gifts.

4) Because the male can never be certain when the female is ovulating, he can't leave her and philander. He has to keep near her at all times.

5) Many primate males are in the habit of killing babies who are not their own. This ensures that the female will only be bringing up his progeny. Perhaps if no male can be certain who is whose offspring, he might be killing one of his own, so the plan is scuppered.

6) Childbirth among humans is very painful and dangerous, principally due to the size of the baby's head pushing through the cervix. Women who were aware of their own ovulation could have avoided copulation during those times, and spared themselves the agony of maternity. Since that line would have died out (through not producing any babies), the remainder were those who couldn't tell if they were ovulating or not.

You have to admire the ingenuity of each of these explanations — all equally plausible and probably unprovable. The choice is yours.

MORAL INDIGNATION IS IN MOST CASES 2 PER CENT MORAL, 48 PER CENT INDIGNATION AND 50 PER CENT ENVY.

(Vittoria de Sica)

The media and infidelity

Why do the media take on such shocked tones when they discover people having affairs? There is clear evidence that philandering happens — all the -ologists are agreed. Zoologists tell us it is normal in the animal kingdom. Anthropologists tell us it happens in all human cultures. Archaeologists tell us it was happening millennia ago. Biologists have seen evidence for it down their microscopes. (Sperm come in two varieties, straight and curly. The straight ones race for the eggs, the curly ones stay behind and enmesh any sperm that follow, presumably the rival's). Evolutionary psychologists tell us there are advantages to it. Infidelity shouldn't surprise or shock us, therefore.

Scandal sheets are not scientific journals, however. What delights them (and us, since we buy them) is the embarrassment of one party and the misery of the other. Science is too cool; what we want is blood and guts. We are tapping into the limbic systems of the unhappy couple and experiencing their guilt and fury vicariously, using our mirror neurons.

IT ISN'T WHAT THEY SAY ABOUT YOU, IT'S WHAT THEY WHISPER.

(Errol Flynn)

Rumour stew

Whether or not we wallow in the public scandals, we're up for it in the pub or at work. We have a healthy appetite for rumour and gossip all day long. The trio of chefs who cook up the rumour stew are our old friends, Messrs Simple, Illogical and Naive.

Simple selects the basic ingredients.
Illogical adds flavour.
Naive does the stirring.

Let's cook up one of the traditional recipes for a rumour –
the 'late nights in the office' dish, or Keith Lorraine.

Simple begins by throwing a number of staple ingredients
in the pot:

One fresh Head of Department (Keith – Illogical says, well
then, he has power and influence, that's tasty).

One spicy secretary (Lorraine – mmmm, says Illogical, she
will be the raising agent).

Three deadlines (The marinade, says Illogical. Keith and
Lorraine will have to work closely on the paperwork for
the promotion).

Simply leave Keith and Lorraine in the marinade for three
weeks. Lots of late nights at the office while they prepare
the campaign.

Add garnish; Keith has been arguing with his wife a lot
recently. He seems quite happy when he's at work, though.
The stew is thickening nicely.

One day Lorraine announces that she's pregnant. The
missing ingredient! Naive stirs, tastes, and no more need be
done. The dish is ready to serve. A beautifully simple recipe,
it will nourish the office rumour mill for weeks.

TRYING TO SQUASH A RUMOUR IS LIKE TRYING TO UNRING A BELL.

(Shana Alexander)

Spicing up the dish

Keith Lorraine is best served with some relish, and must not be taken with a pinch of salt. The secret ingredient is secrecy itself. Nothing adds zest better than strictest confidence. Each time it is served the taste is more exotic, the texture is more free of uncomfortable lumps (like the fact that Lorraine is happily married and everyone knew she and her husband were trying for a baby). So nobody must know. 'You must promise not to tell a SOUL!' Saying that will give the rumour wings.

What would happen if Keith or Lorraine discovered the rumour? That would be awful, like opening the oven door on a soufflé – all the heat would be lost, the dish would sink and entirely lose its flavour. Nobody would swallow it.

TO AVOID MISTAKES AND REGRETS, ALWAYS CONSULT YOUR WIFE BEFORE ENGAGING IN A FLIRTATION.

(E. W. Howe)

Fear of infidelity

There is a difference between men and women in their fear of infidelity. According to surveys, women are concerned that their man might be forming an emotional attachment, whether or not actual sex is taking place. Men are concerned about whether their women are indulging in sex, regardless of emotional attachment. There is a guiding hand behind these differences. Men want to bring up their own children. They don't want to waste their time bringing up someone else's. They don't want their partners risking pregnancy by sleeping around. For women, the fear is that the provider will not be there to do the providing if his heart belongs to someone else.

Is this difference due to circumstances, or is it a fundamental difference between women and men? It seems from the research that the fear doesn't diminish for the woman when she has an independent income, or for the man if she is using contraception. This suggests that the difference is hard-wired, evolved long ago, and will not be modified any time soon.

DOUBTS ARE MORE CRUEL THAN THE WORST OF TRUTHS.

(Molière)

Jealousy I

Jealousy is the dark side of love. Stories of jealousy, violence and bloody revenge are numerous enough to keep the bookshops stocked for centuries; indeed they already have done. Such human cataclysms are to be found in their pages! Such crimes of passion! People murder the most loved person in their life *because* they love them. Confronted by a crime of passion, many of us say, why did he let his emotions carry him away? Why couldn't she be more rational? If only we could cure jealousy. But jealousy is the opposite side of the coin to love. Take away jealousy and love dies, because the same hormones feed them both.

If we were all thoroughly rational about our choice of partner we would pick the most appropriate candidate from the available stock in a nice systematic way, with application forms, bank statements and medical reports to hand, selecting the one that scored highest on the pairing formula on p. 68 (same neighbourhood, same cultural background, income and religion, same wrist size, middle finger ratio and inter-occular distance, who remind us at key points of our parents, etc.). Points could be totalled and the winner could be married, without any wasted passion.

The problem is, if we met someone better qualified years later we might leave our long-standing spouse and any children forthwith and set up afresh with the new, better qualified partner. It would be the rational thing to do. For strictly rational people, therefore, bonding is a problem. The glue of irrational love is what holds two people together, and what causes the pain when they split. If you aren't jealous, you weren't in love in the first place. So it goes.

LOVE LOOKS THROUGH A TELESCOPE; JEALOUSY, THROUGH A MICROSCOPE.

(Josh Billings)

Jealousy II

At times of crisis we seem to gain superhuman powers. We have heard tales of people displaying extraordinary strength in a battle or lightning reactions to save their child. Love and jealousy are also 'crises', hormonally speaking; both love and jealousy result in the brain's neurons being flooded with the 'accelerator' hormone of adrenaline, among others, so in both cases perception is heightened. In the case of love, the lover sees brighter colours, hears richer music and sees the very best in their partner. In the case of jealousy, we suddenly discover that, like Superman, we have extra abilities: X-ray vision, super-sensitive ears, mind-reading powers. The jealous eye spots invisible changes in body language, the jealous ear hears tiny nuances of speech, which might betray guilt.

With lowered serotonin levels, obsessive-compulsive behaviour is guaranteed. Every detail of our best-beloved is analysed with forensic thoroughness. If you are on the receiving end of this examination it can be unnerving. Your nervousness is picked up, of course, and that makes Superman more suspicious, because it looks a little as if you have something to hide. That makes you more nervous, and so a 'feedback loop' is created which can only spiral one way. It's going to be a bad few days.

FOOL ME ONCE, SHAME ON YOU; FOOL ME TWICE, SHAME ON ME.

Suspicion

After the affair is discovered and the rival beaten off, the loving processes go into reverse. The fantasy that drove our love, that allowed us to see only the good in our partner, that fantasy has gone, to be replaced with an entirely different fantasy: the one-time lover turns into a dedicated policeman trying to uncover the next crime before it happens. Whether they know it or not the ex-con is being watched a lot more carefully now.

For the aggrieved wife, the three S.I.N. sisters are her constant companions; Simple, Illogical and Naive are now working on another campaign. Instead of seeing everything through the pink lens of the telescope, they are peering down the dark tunnel of a microscope, finding things to be suspicious about in every twitch and nuance. Simple now knows that all men are only after one thing. Illogical assumes that all his conversations with the opposite sex are chat-ups. Naive guesses that, when she phones him, if he doesn't answer immediately it's because THEY ARE AT IT. The obsession of jealousy leads women to check their men's pockets regularly and secretly skim through their mail. If he says a word he has never used before, the dogs of doubt begin to bark: where did he pick that up from? For their part, men have a history of locking their women away, abusing and beating them, and of course crimes of passion. It's hard, it's very hard to call this love by other means.

NOW HATRED IS BY FAR THE LONGEST PLEASURE; MEN LOVE IN HASTE, BUT THEY DETEST AT LEISURE.

(Lord Byron)

Post-traumatic stress disorder

When a couple 'split', the physical separation is easily accomplished, but the mental process is much slower. You now have two completely different sets of emotion for everything you shared – friends, family, Christmases . . . it's a long list after all this time. One emotion is happiness, the other is pain. How should you remember things? The brain is confused and the result is thoroughly, viscerally agonizing. You are suffering a mild form of post-traumatic stress disorder (PTSD).

(To take an example from another area, there is a parallel with simple giddiness caused by spinning round too many times. When the messages from the balance organs of the middle ears and the messages from the eyes conflict with each other – one saying that you are still spinning while the other says you are not – it creates a feeling of nausea. During PTSD your conflicting emotions clash inside your head, creating much less manageable contradictions.)

PTSD shows in general restlessness, insomnia, sudden mood swings, depression and nightmares. Stress hormones are raised, and anxiety levels higher. The mind has to make sense of the event, which it will do by rewriting the entire story . . .

NOTHING FIXES A THING SO INTENSELY IN THE MEMORY AS THE WISH TO FORGET IT.

(Montaigne)

Rewriting the back-story

Memories are not as permanently fixed as we believe them to be, but can be recast later in the light of new information. That enormous bunch of flowers he gave you was remembered not just as an array of plants that smelled, but as a thing of joy, a symbol of devotion. Well, that will have to be reassessed now, won't it? He had just got back from a steamy late-night session with that woman. This was not 'devotion' but 'guilt'.

Everything is different now. The brain has a lot of work to do. It seems the whole memory bank will have to be re-labelled. All his pleasantries were nothing but propaganda. The gifts? Bribes! The work in your brain goes on all week, 24/7, hence the sleepless, spook-filled nights. You are rewriting the entire back-story.

Some of the new back-story doesn't work. You want to reconfigure him as a very devil, but you recall that the fiend was actually mostly considerate, often generous, witty and popular with all your friends – just too popular with one of them, that's all. It is these paradoxes which keep you awake the longest. Eventually you must sort them out, so that the story you tell yourself is internally consistent, even at the expense of actual truth. Perhaps he was an innocent, seduced by a scheming witch. Perhaps he never loved you, and you were too busy loving him to notice. Perhaps – horrors! – it was your fault.

THE WALLS WE BUILD AROUND US TO KEEP SADNESS OUT ALSO KEEP OUT THE JOY.

(Jim Rohn)

Withdrawal

Withdrawal from the world is a danger after a relationship fails. Being cuckolded brings with it the stigma of being second-rate, and now second-hand. You may well feel intense loss of self-esteem. Your judgement has taken a good knocking. Self-protective behaviour will guard you against more hurt; you can avoid pain by shunning people, but it is not the path to recovery. You need to find your own people. Your family and friends will help to comfort you. The best revenge, says the Talmud, is to live well. Friends and family, these are the bonds that you had before the bond that you've lost. Evolution has ensured that there will always be an easy empathy to be found. Their mirror neurons will help them share your grief. Of course they will tell you there are plenty more fish in the sea. And they will be right, even though you don't feel like getting out the fishing tackle again.

But your future is not in your hands anyway, it lies with your instincts. The evolutionary force that brought you here doesn't take long to get back in the driving seat. The revving up for sex is strong enough in the end to drive you out into the marketplace again. And there you will find someone who thinks you are special.

THE WHEEL TURNS
FULL CIRCLE

**A SECOND MARRIAGE IS THE TRIUMPH OF
HOPE OVER EXPERIENCE.**

(Samuel Johnson)

All over again

The strangest thing is that when people eventually open
themselves up to love again, it is so often a repeat of the last
time. Like the princess who has been kissing frogs for
several years without success deciding that the best way
forward is to kiss yet more frogs, people often keep going
for the same kind of lover that was so disastrous last time.
When this happens we can blame that list of unconscious
requirements on p. 68. You are driven to search out the
same qualities once more, so what is to stop you making
the same mistake again? Nothing. History repeats itself.

In extreme cases this can be quite startling: the ex-wife
of an abusive drunkard chucks all his belonging in the
street, changes the locks, gets a restraining order to stop

him throwing beer bottles through the window, starts afresh. Her friends breathe a sigh of relief, then stare aghast as she introduces her new boyfriend – a convivial extrovert with attitude, that is to say, an abusive drunkard.

FEW THINGS ARE MORE SATISFYING THAN SEEING YOUR CHILDREN HAVE TEENAGERS OF THEIR OWN.

(Doug Larson)

We all want babies. Girls get broody when they're three, seriously broody when they're thirteen and unstoppable when they're thirty. (OK, that's a bit of a broad sweep, but watching a three-year-old girl with a doll makes you realize parenthood is no accident when it happens.) When they do eventually have babies, women find out about the power of bonding all over again. When the baby suckles, or massages the breast, oxytocin is released in the mother. The father, too, bonds with baby, and afresh with mother, and the family is united in the kind of hormonal haze which Mum and Dad remember from when they first met and fell in love.

Now, all you have to do is bring up baby . . .

Remember your useless parents? You didn't throw away their telephone number, did you? You need them now. Baby is giving trouble, crying all night and day. You are dead tired, your partner is working split shifts, trying to earn the money, and is tetchy when not asleep. Thank goodness Mum and Dad can baby-sit.

Ten years later you still need them. Sonny likes to spend the odd week with Grandpa and Grandma, which is great because it gives you a break. In fact Sonny seems to enjoy their company more than yours. In fact, truth be told, Sonny doesn't appreciate you quite as much as he should, in your opinion, considering all the sacrifices you make for him.

Five years on, Sonny thinks you are the pits, the ungrateful wretch. He drifts around the house – your house, not his, YOURS – mumbling incoherently, dropping filthy socks all over the place, going out at night without saying where he's off to, or at least not in any language recognized on earth. God knows what he gets up to, but it's almost certainly illegal or immoral.

What is happening to this country? It wasn't like this when you were young, was it?

Why do Grandma and Grandpa have such immovable smirks on their faces when they visit these days?

CONCLUSION

Murphy's Law was originally devised at a crash-testing station in America as a precautionary mantra, to make sure every possible nut, bolt and rivet of the test equipment was checked and double checked.

WHATEVER CAN GO WRONG WILL GO WRONG

The crew would repeat this as they made sure nothing could go wrong. Personal relationships are too wild to be strapped up or bolted down. They can go off the rails, hit the buffers, or be over the moon. When they crash, they do so spectacularly.

Love is what made the world go round from the first bacterium onwards; either 'lurve' – our human, dreamy, drooly, syrupy version – or *Deroceras gorgonium*'s single, exquisite second, or the simple adherence of one amoeba to another has been a fundamental force of nature and will continue to be so until the earth makes its coitus with the sun.

What we really want in a partner is absolutely clear. Women want men who are tough but soft, commanding but willing to listen to advice, who will keep out from under their feet but always be there when needed, with an illustrious job that pays well but plenty of spare time for the kids.

Men want a woman to be attractive but not to anyone else, to be an earth-mother and dote on the children but have an executive career in her spare time, to have a grasp of finance and scheduling . . . but not too much.

Enjoy the search. Everyone will be losers most of the time, hopefully all will be learners all the time. Most will be winners some of the time. And in the meantime, remember:

IF YOU CAN'T BE WITH THE ONE YOU LOVE, LOVE THE ONE YOU'RE WITH.

(Stephen Stills)

APPENDIX I

THE EVOLUTION OF EMOTIONS

NOBODY KNOWS THE AGE OF THE HUMAN RACE, BUT EVERYBODY AGREES THAT IT IS OLD ENOUGH TO KNOW BETTER.

An emotion is a driving force caused by hormones. For example there is the emotion of disgust when we smell a pint of milk that has gone off which makes us jerk our head away, or the craving hunger that makes us reach out when we smell freshly cooked blueberry muffins with cream topping. In an earlier time the cyanobacteria in the Archaean era had more modest tastes and motivations. After all, they were the first to arrive at the party, some three and a half billion years before the evolution of the muffin, and were the first life-form on the planet. Yet these simple, one-celled creatures were able to move away from toxins in the water and towards the light. We cannot say they were 'disgusted' by the toxins or that they 'craved' the light, but they behaved for all the world as if that was the case. Their driving forces were the ancestors of our emotions, and the chemicals that made them do it were the forerunners of our hormones.

Teamwork

Those proto-hormones proved wonderfully versatile when teamwork was invented. A contemporary of cyanobacteria evolved the ability to work together. The poetically named slime mould, *dictyostelia*, has survived through to modern times. It can be found coating rocks or tree stumps with a thin slimy (hence the name) layer. The slime is actually a family of over 100,000 individual amoebas. Each amoeba is autonomous and like cyanobacteria will react to chemical changes around it by moving towards desirable conditions and avoiding unpleasant ones. But at certain times a remarkable change occurs, which cyanobacteria can't match. The whole amoeba colony will suddenly stop what it's doing, as if everyone had received a signal from some kind of central control, and start to migrate towards the centre of the colony. The amoebas form into a long, slug-like body called a pseudo-plasmodium. This slug starts to display distinct signs of personality now. It will wander across the rock in search of more food, and if it can't find any the amoebas that make up the slug will work together again to form a stalk and release spores. But there is no central control for all this – no brain. The whole thing has been achieved by simple chemical signals exuded by the amoebas.

Multi-cellular organisms

All the amoebas in a slime mould are the same – in fact they are all clones of each other, so a certain amount of harmony could be expected. Can the same chemical signalling system deal with more complex animals? The next step up the ladder towards the richly subtle creature that is you would be the sponge.

Sponges first appeared 2 billion years after cyanobacteria and *dictyostelia* (about 1.5 billion years ago). They are colonies of up to nine different creatures, each with a specialist skill, which combined together make the sponge a very efficient being. For instance, sclerocytes create stiffened spikes for structure and defence, porocytes allow water in, and all over the surface of the sponge sit choanocytes each with a whip-like flagellum which wafts food into the sponge. It is extraordinary to watch the choanocytes in action. All the flagella move in synchrony, like the legs of a millipede. Yet there is no central control; if you put the sponge through a blender, the resulting mush will reform itself into a fully working sponge again, with all the cells in a different order, but all beating in harmony with their new neighbours. The coordination happens by a simple chemical signal passing from cell to cell, just like the slime mould.

The emotional life of sponges

How much emotion can you get out of a sponge? You just liquidized it, but it didn't scream in pain, or bite you in anger, or make a break for the door. No emotions there, you say. But the chemical signals which drive the choanocytes are the distant cousins of the chemical signals that cause you to fall in love. The basic desires of that sponge – to feed, to avoid unpleasantness and to make babies, which it can do by releasing sperm and eggs into the water – these urges are similar to the basic human urges known in the psychology world as the four Fs: Feeding, Fighting, Fleeing and Fornication (to spare the blushes). And the proto-hormones are controlling it just like modern hormones. Emotions and the hormones that cause them have been around in one shape or another since life began.

Brains

There was one more major advance to be made in the field of hormones. You see, chemical signals are a bit random. They diffuse in all directions, and quite slowly at that. The evolution of a nervous system led to a great leap forward in the animal world. Now hormones could send their instructions fast, and to an exact spot. It was a jellyfish, which boasted the first nerves, about 600 million years ago, and it could really get about in style thanks to its jelly-wide-web – a sort of Cambrian bend-and-stretch limo. But it didn't stop there. Nerves were such a good idea that they kept on evolving – into eyes, ears, touch sensors, then brains to coordinate all this – in other words an entire nervous system, though still controlled by the hormones that started the whole thing off in the first place. In the modern brain, your hormones sit in the control room at the centre (the limbic system), and the rest of the brain and nervous system sits around it ready to do its bidding.

Separate animals

Another great leap forward was actually a leap in all directions. Animals could exude chemical signals into the water which wafted into one of its neighbour's new-fangled smell organs and caused them to change their direction, just like their ancestors, the *dictyostelia*. Even better, when eyes and ears and lateral lines (for reading water pressure signals or electrical signals) evolved, it became possible to perform coordinated actions between thousands of them across huge distances. The result of this is all around us today; schools of fish, flocks of birds, prides of lions, etc. And tribes of humans, of course. Why would it be useful to go around in groups? For the same reason that it was useful in slime moulds: it helps you to travel, hunt, breed, avoid predators, and share muffins.

We humans do a lot, a very great lot, of teamwork, using our mirror neurons (see pp. 4, 102) to send and receive signals through sounds and visual cues. We also do a lot of invisible, unconscious signalling, through body language, micro-gestures and – an unexplored area this – by chemical signalling through pheromones, (see p. 88), MHC molecules (see p. 91) and a variety of other odours which science has yet to investigate fully. We watch, we listen, we smell and we modify; this is the legacy of the hormone.

APPENDIX 2

MURPHY'S LAWS OF LOVE

Introduction

Whatever can go wrong will go wrong.   ix

Chapter 1: Roll, Pitch and Yaw

Call it a clan, call it a network, call it a tribe, call it a family.
Whatever you call it, whoever you are, you need one.   4
(Jane Howard)

I don't have to look up my family tree, because I know
that I'm the sap.   6
(Fred Allen)

We are faced with insurmountable opportunities!   7
(Charlie Brown)

Custom meets us at the cradle and leaves us only at the
tomb.   9
(Robert Ingersoll)

A boy becomes an adult three years before his parents think
he does, and about two years after he thinks he does.   11
(Lewis B. Hershey)

My life has a superb cast, but I can't figure out the plot.   13
(Ashleigh Brilliant)

Adolescence: a stage between infancy and adultery.   14
(Ambrose Bierce)

A man who carries a cat by the tail learns something he
can learn in no other way.   17
(Mark Twain)

Experience is the name everyone gives to his mistakes.   19
(Oscar Wilde)

Try again. Fail again. Fail better.   19
(Samuel Beckett)

Chapter 2: Men and Women: Gulf Wars

Women who seek to be equal with men lack ambition.   24
(Timothy Leary)

Women have their faults
Men have only two
Everything they say
And everything they do.   26

The world can be divided into two sorts of people:
those who divide the world into two sorts of people
and those who don't.   27

<u>Three</u> wise men – are you serious?   28

Give a woman an inch and she thinks she's a ruler.   29

The only difference between men and boys is the cost of
their toys.   30

If it can't be fixed by duct tape or WD-40, it's a female
problem.   32
(Jason Love)

Every woman is wrong until she cries, and then she is right –
instantly.   33
(Thomas Chandler Haliburton)

Sure God created man before woman. But then you always
make a rough draft before the final masterpiece.   34

Never argue with a woman when she's tired – or rested.   35

Whatever women do they must do twice as well as men
to be thought half as good. Luckily, this is not difficult.   36
(Charlotte Whitton)

On one issue at least, both women and men agree – they
both distrust women.   38
(H. L. Mencken)

Both men and women distrust men.   38

Nobody will ever win the battle of the sexes. There's
just too much fraternizing with the enemy.   38
(Henry Kissinger)

Chapter 3: Courting Disaster

Fashion is what you adopt when you don't know who
you are.   41
(Quentin Crisp)

When people are free to do as they please, they usually imitate
each other.   43
(Eric Hoffer)

To be natural is such a very difficult pose to keep up.   44
(Oscar Wilde)

'Know thyself'? If I knew myself, I'd run away.   45
(Johann Wolfgang von Goethe)

Plain women know more about men than beautiful
ones do.   46
(Katharine Hepburn)

To find out a girl's faults, praise her to her girlfriends.   47
(Benjamin Franklin)

The first time you buy a house you see how pretty the
paint is and buy it. The second time you look to see if the
basement has termites. It's the same with men.   49
(Lupe Velez)

Brains are an asset, if you hide them.   50
(Mae West)

Men don't make passes at female smart-asses.   52
(Lettie Cottin Pogrebin)

Beauty is skin deep; ugly goes right to the bone.   53

Chapter 4: Nice Assessment

My problem lies in reconciling my gross habits with my net income.   70
(Errol Flynn)

If you feel romantic, laddy,
Let me warn you right from the start
That my heart belongs to daddy
And my daddy belongs to my heart.   71
(Cole Porter)

You should make a point of trying every experience once, excepting incest and folk-dancing.   73
(Sir Arnold Bax)

Familiarity breeds contempt.   74

I believe in getting into hot water; it keeps you clean.   75
(G. K. Chesterton)

Chapter 5: Slithery Slopes

Love is only a dirty trick played on us to achieve continuation of the species.   77
(W. Somerset Maugham)

There is no difference between a wise man and a fool when they fall in love.   78

Do you believe in love at first sight, or do I have to walk past you again?   79

The only true love is love at first sight; second sight dispels it.   81
(Israel Zangwill)

A hen is only an egg's way of making another egg.   83
(Samuel Butler)

It upsets women to be, or not to be, stared at hungrily.   84
(Mignon McLaughlin)

It is better to be looked over than overlooked.   85

If you get them by the balls, their hearts and minds will
follow.   87
(President Lyndon B. Johnson)

Love unlocks doors and opens windows that weren't
even there before.   88
(Mignon McLaughlin)

It is absurd to divide people into good and bad. People are
either charming or tedious.   89
(Oscar Wilde)

The one you fancy never fancies you.   90

We all worry about the population explosion, but we don't
worry about it at the right time.   93
(Arthur Hoppe)

Live fast, die young – live slow, die anyway.   94

Forget love. I'd rather fall in chocolate.   96

Nothing takes the taste out of peanut butter quite like
unrequited love.   97
(Charlie Brown)

Chapter 6: The Nitty Gritty

Life without sex might be safer but it would be
unbearably dull. It is the sex instinct which makes
women seem beautiful, which they are once in a blue
moon, and men seem wise and brave, which they never
are at all. Throttle it, denaturalize it, take it away, and
human existence would be reduced to the prosaic,
laborious, boresome, imbecile level of life in an anthill.   111
(H. L. Mencken)

Love is an exploding cigar we willingly smoke.   112
(Lynda Barry)

Coito, ergo sum.   113

Sex: the pleasure is momentary, the position ridiculous,
and the expense damnable.   114
(Lord Chesterfield)

What is the difference between men and women? A
woman wants one man to satisfy her every need, and a
man wants every woman to satisfy his one need.   116

A hard man is good to find.   119
(Mae West)

Literature is mostly about having sex and not much about
having children; life is the other way around.   120
(David Lodge)

Nymphomaniac: a woman as obsessed with sex as an
average man.   122
(Mignon McLaughlin)

Life in Lubbock, Texas, taught me two things: one is
that God loves you and you're going to burn in hell.
The other is that sex is the most awful, filthy thing on
earth and you should save it for someone you love.   123
(Butch Hancock)

A big difference between sex for money and sex for free
is that sex for money usually costs less.   124
(Brendan Francis)

Never sleep with anyone crazier than yourself.   125

Love is a matter of chemistry, sex is a matter of physics. 126

The only part the heart plays in love is to mark the
mid-point between brain and the groin.   128

Life is a sexually transmitted disease.   129

Chapter 7: Wedding Prescience

If it were not for the presents, elopement would be
preferable.   132
(G. Ade)

It doesn't really matter whom one marries; one is sure
to find out next morning that it was somebody else.   134
(Will Rogers)

All marriages are happy. It's the living together afterward
that causes all the trouble.   136
(Raymond Hull)

In every marriage more than a week old, there are
grounds for divorce. The trick is to find, and continue to
find, grounds for marriage.   137
(Robert Anderson)

Successful marriage requires falling in love many times,
always with the same person.   138
(Mignon McLaughlin)

How can a woman be expected to be happy with a man
who insists on treating her as if she were a normal human
being?   139
(Oscar Wilde)

The course of true anything never does run smooth.   140
(Samuel Butler)

One advantage of marriage is that, when you fall out of
love with him or he falls out of love with you, it keeps
you together until you fall in again.   141
(Judith Viorst)

Chapter 8: Playing Away

Monogamy leaves a lot to be desired.   145

You know that the Tasmanians, who never committed
adultery, are now extinct.   145
(W. Somerset Maugham)

Infidelity is the application of democracy to love.   147
(H. L. Mencken)

To our mistresses and wives. May they never meet.   148

Motherhood is a matter of fact, fatherhood is a matter of opinion.   149

Moral indignation is in most cases 2 per cent moral, 48 per cent indignation and 50 per cent envy.   151
(Vittoria de Sica)

It isn't what they say about you, it's what they whisper.   152
(Errol Flynn)

Trying to squash a rumour is like trying to unring a bell.   154
(Shana Alexander)

To avoid mistakes and regrets, always consult your wife before engaging in a flirtation.   155
(E. W. Howe)

Doubts are more cruel than the worst of truths.   156
(Molière)

Love looks through a telescope; jealousy, through a microscope.   158
(Josh Billings)

Fool me once, shame on you; fool me twice, shame on me.   160

Now hatred is by far the longest pleasure;
Men love in haste, but they detest at leisure.   161
(Lord Byron)

FURTHER READING

The books below are all eminently readable, and all take the subject of human emotions, sexuality and relationships much further than I can in this book. Read them all.

Simon Baron-Cohen, *The Essential Difference*. London: Penguin, 2004

Patrick Bateson, *Mate Choice*. Cambridge: Cambridge University Press, 1983

Susan Blackmore, *The Meme Machine*. Oxford: Oxford University Press, 2000

Bill Bryson, *A Short History of Nearly Everything*. London: Black Swan, 2004

Richard Dawkins, *The Selfish Gene*. Oxford: Oxford University Press, 1989

Jared Diamond, *The Rise and Fall of the Third Chimpanzee*. London: Vintage, 1992

Robin Dunbar, *The Human Story: A New History of Mankind's Evolution*. London: Faber and Faber, 2004

Felipe Fernández-Armesto, *So You Think You're Human?: A Brief History of Humankind.* Oxford: Oxford University Press, 2005

Elisabeth Lloyd, *The Case of Female Orgasm: Bias in the Science of Evolution.* Cambridge, MA: Harvard University Press, 2005

Geoffrey Miller, *The Mating Mind: How Sexual Choice Shaped the Evolution of Human Nature.* London: Vintage, 2001

Simon Pinker, *How the Mind Works.* London: Penguin, 1999

Robert Winston, *Human Instinct.* London: Bantam, 2002

Translation of Notorious B.I.G. rap posted on:
http://www.bizbag.com/Misc%20articles/Rap%20
Lyrics%20Translated.htm

WHY THE TOAST ALWAYS LANDS BUTTER SIDE DOWN

Richard Robinson

The real scientific reasons why everything always goes wrong ...

Start looking for Murphy's Law, and you'll find it everywhere. Buses go round in threes, the queue you join always goes slowest, when your hands are full your nose starts to itch, you think of 10 important things to remember just as you are falling asleep ...

Can there ever be a rational explanation?

The answers turn out to be one part scientific to three parts psychology. The world has changed a lot in the last 4000 years, but our brains haven't. So, again and again we find our reactions are just plain out of date.

- Why do you take the same wrong turn every single time?
- Why, when you lose something, do you keep looking in the same place over and over?
- And why is it suddenly there the twentieth time you look?

365 WAYS TO CHANGE THE WORLD
Michael Norton

You want to change the world? Of course you do. But where do you begin?

Packed with ideas from leading campaign organisations for conservation and social justice, this ingenious handbook shows how even the smallest changes can impact on your home, your community, your country and the wider world.

It suggests one action for every day of the year, most of which can be planned or done from home. All the activities are inspiring and most are fun and easy to do, including:

- Support trade justice: buy fair-trade tea and coffee
- Avoid landfills: 'freecycle' stuff you no longer need
- Sow the seeds of a green revolution: become a guerrilla gardener
- Go unshopping: list ten things you'll never buy again
- Do something about poverty: organise a 'Dinner for Life'

Subscribe to receive *read more*, your monthly newsletter from Penguin Australia. As a *read more* subscriber you'll receive sneak peeks of new books, be kept up to date with what's hot, have the opportunity to meet your favourite authors, download reading guides for your book club, receive special offers, be in the running to win exclusive subscriber-only prizes, plus much more.

Visit penguin.com.au to subscribe.